Let's Do This!
HEARTCENTRED LEADERSHIP

A NEW PARADIGM OF ENTREPRENEURS

COMPILED BY LAURA ELIZABETH

MAVEN PRESS

A catalogue record for this
work is available from the
National Library of Australia

National Library of Australia Catalogue-in-Publication data:
Let's Do This! Heartcentred Leadership/Laura Elizabeth

ISBN: 978-0-6453230-0-9
(Paperback)

ISBN: 978-0-6453230-1-6
(Ebook)

FOREWORD

In unity, we honour and pay our respects to the custodians of Whadjuk Noongar Boodjar country, the lands on which this book was first seeded.

We pay our respects to the Elders both past and present and to those emerging.

The stories within these pages may contain sensitive content and/ or memories of loved ones who have passed on, which may activate a response within you.

Please read with awareness and care.

CONTENTS

INTRODUCTION

Magic happens when women come together.

In this book, nineteen women impart their stories of triumph and tribulation as they navigate that inner voice calling them to a higher purpose. They have committed to being seen in their real, raw, vulnerable truth – to inspire you on your own journey. To remind you that you are not alone.

What does it mean to be a leader and why is heart-centredness so important in this day and age as an entrepreneur?

Whether you are an expert in your field or just beginning to branch into your niche as a heart-centred leader, these stories will inspire you to dig deep, find your truth and believe in yourself.

Cherie Melina

FAILURE

What is failure? The Oxford Dictionary defines failure as "1. Lack of success; 2. The neglect or omission of expected or required action". Expected? Hmm, that's interesting! To whom's expectations am I meeting? Don't expectations change and morph depending on who's ego is aligning to them?

If failure is not meeting an expectation, then well, we're all failures, aren't we? And as for 'lack of success', isn't that defined by our expectations as well? In business, we are expected to meet certain obligations and criteria. Bills must be paid; Wages, super, taxes, rent, stock, loans, credit cards, etc. But what happens when your outgoings far outweigh your income and you fail to meet these expectations that we are all obliged to meet? In my experience, that's when fear steps in, panic starts and the ego has all the answers. All with the intention of avoiding failure.

Have you ever had that feeling in the pit of your stomach of pure panic, alongside sleepless nights and thoughts swimming around in your head of different scenarios and solutions to one simple (yet not so simple) thing – money? I've woken in the middle of the night with panic attacks about money. I've buried my emotions deep down pretending that everything was okay. That next week, next month, would be better. That I would trade out of the mess I had gotten myself into. That the credit cards, overdrafts, personal loans, superannuation, BAS, tax, rent and suppliers would get paid down a little more next week. Reminding myself that the most important thing was that I had paid my staff, and that they were happy. And as long as they were there, they could help me trade out of this situation. I could give them a pep talk, and put the fire under them a little. Get them to upsell and work a little harder.

But then I'd remember that the city was so quiet. The bookings simply weren't there; I couldn't drag people off the street. I began to ask myself – *Where did I go wrong? What am I doing? How do I get out of this? CLOSE THE DOORS!* I would hear myself say. But I couldn't do it. What would I do for work? How would I earn money? I couldn't get a 'regular' job; I'd been self-employed for fifteen years. I wouldn't get paid enough from a regular job to keep my house, or keep my son in private school, or keep my car ...

So there I was; unable to accept what I had created or accept responsibility for where the business was financially, and unable to surrender my attachments to things that I held onto so tightly. I had FAILED; I'd neglected and omitted the expected and required action.

I had so many people offer their help during this time. I had a client, who is a corporate lawyer, set up a meeting for me to discuss liquidation. This terrified me. That word, LIQUIDATION. If you close your eyes for just a moment and connect to the word 'liquidation', what does that conjure up for you? I know right, FAILURE. Cemented and sealed. Forced to accept that this is where I'd ended up – no, thanks. I still believed I could 'fix' this situation. In this case, I didn't like the look of the help I was being offered, so I turned it down.

Another client offered to pay my son's school fees with her belief that education was of the utmost importance in life. He was only halfway through year nine at a very prestigious college, and she was committed to paying three and a half years of his school fees. As hard as it was to accept, it was still a lot easier than the alternative; sending him to a public school. OMG, I couldn't do that – *He'd be eaten alive*, I thought (I can laugh at this now). So this help, I gladly accepted.

Instead of closing the doors to my business, as my guidance was screaming at me to do, I decided to put the business on the market. I enlisted a business broker to assist with the sale and advertised it privately on several online avenues. I then decided to borrow a huge amount of money from one of those online loan sharks that deposits funds into your account within twenty-four hours, to stay afloat while I waited for a buyer. You see, again, that to me was better than the alternative. I couldn't close the doors on the business that was my blood, sweat and tears for twenty years. All around me, businesses were closing down, including some big names. I was watching the CBD dive into a pit of despair. *For Lease* signs on empty shops were more common than store shop fronts. My attachment was so deep and so strong, I just couldn't seem to detach and set myself free. Maybe it was because I wasn't educated enough on all of my options, or I was a slave to my ego and fears. It was eating me up from the inside out, and I'd have days where the burden was so much that I couldn't even imagine a life without it. It was becoming part of me; nestling itself into my being and into my cells. What you become is truly what you attract.

I, of all people, should have known this. I was about three years into a self-mastery course called The Masters' Way, channelled by In'Easa mabu Ishtar. A course about mastering your energies, teaching you to take responsibility for all you create. I was learning how to let go of all that did not serve me on my divine path and learning to work with and embrace separation consciousness, or shadow, as some will call it. I had been having deep healing sessions with my mentor and teacher to try and shift the energy that I was holding and that was consuming me. I even had her come to my shop to do a healing on the space. I remember tuning into the frequency of the energy of the space, and OMG – it was so stifled by the low density consciousness of the city. So much intensity of the ego; the 'have-tos', 'need-tos' and constant striving to meet the expectations of others. It felt like a huge muddy puddle with souls being swallowed up by a life driven by ego. When I had made the decision in 2013 to become a student in The Masters' Way, this is when my business had started to reflect the imbalances to me. I was choosing a path of enlightenment and the path of the ego was slowly starting to peel itself away.

My business was a very flash-looking beauty salon, smack bang in the middle of Perth CBD. I began working in this very salon when I was eighteen years old, and my old boss likes to remind me of my job interview, when she asked where I saw myself in the future. Apparently I answered with, "I'm going to buy this place one day," and that I did. When I bought it in 2005, it was very outdated and run down; a typical late eighties beauty parlour. I borrowed money from my parents and refinanced our home to buy it and renovate it, and it went off with a BANG. It was tiny though, with only three rooms and no floor-to-ceiling walls so it wasn't soundproof at all, which made it difficult to do a massage or a facial, which were becoming more and more sought after. So by the time my lease was to be renewed, I was pulsed (and I will use this term frequently) to search for a larger space.

My old boss (who worked upstairs in a menswear store) had come to see me one day with news of a newly renovated space, that the salon had once previously occupied, becoming available to lease. She had even introduced me to the managing director of the building and put in a good word for me. It was from here that I began to create a beast! We wheeled and dealed, and I borrowed more money from my parents. Before I knew it, I was elbows-deep in designing a HUGE purpose-built salon, on a rather generous budget. I was project managing, designing, dreaming up logos, treatments and brands to sell, and wow, was it exciting. Oh, and I should probably mention that at this point I was now also a single mumma providing for her young boy. *What an opportunity*, I thought.

I had a fabulous team of girls and the new place began to tick over a tidy sum of money. I had it all. The sports car, nice clothes, fancy friends, my own little house, a cute little boy, travel, money in the bank, cocktails on the weekends and a steady stream of good-looking fellas to be seen out with. Until one day I realised just how lonely I was, and how none of this stuff was really bringing me joy. From the outside looking in, I was the luckiest girl in the world. But my soul was so lost. I was looking outside of myself constantly to fill this gap within me.

And that's when I met Daz. A drive-through bottle shop attendant, of all people (he doesn't work there now), and we started going out. There was a lot more to this guy than I gave him credit for. It was at the same time that we'd hooked up that I had decided to do The Masters' Way course. It was once a week at my teacher's house in Roleystone, and I lived in Embleton at the time so Daz used to come over and look after my son while I went to school. Eventually Daz and I decided to move in together and start looking for a place that we could call our own. At this point, my business was lagging a little, so selling my house and taking a bit of the equity made sense so I could pay down some overheads. I had credit cards maxed out, overdrafts used to the eyeballs, personal loans, tax debt and I also owed creditors; but I still felt in control and confident in trading out. Plus, the business was in a family trust, so I knew that me and my personal assets would be fine. Nothing could really go wrong.

We ended up buying a beautiful house in Roleystone, of all places. I'd only been driving up there once a week for the past two years, so again we were pulsed to buy this house. We lived there together as a family unit and I drove to the city every day for work. At this point, I was doing all the mastery work, mantras and self-love required of me to become more enlightened, but my business seemed to be doing worse than ever. I knew I needed to take action. I would drive past a cute little village on the high-way on my way to the train station every day and see a little beauty salon set amongst a picturesque setting. *Mmm, one day*, I would say to myself.

Once a year, within the self-mastery course that I was doing, the creator of this work would organise a retreat; usually somewhere fabulous overseas, when travel was still a thing. I opened an email one day and saw that this particular retreat would be held in Hawaii on the Big Island, and again, I felt this pulse that I had to go. I knew I couldn't afford it but I knew it was what I needed to do to maybe even save my business. There was a really strong urge to attend. So with the payment options available and by rejigging a few things, it was decided – I was going to Hawaii. But OMG, talk about universal resistance … My flights were cancelled and I was stranded in Melbourne with no money. I called my mentor in Perth sobbing and she ended up fixing everything for me; apparently this was to be a lesson in accepting help and opening my heart to receive. So, off I went, after an overnight stay in Melbourne.

Once in Hawaii, we did a lot of work on opening to receive guidance, support and assistance from many parts of our multidimensional selves. It was, in fact, two weeks of being surrounded by like-minded souls, in a group heart, on a Lemurian portal. Very powerful (and even if you don't quite know what a Lemurian portal is, it still sounds pretty powerful, doesn't it!). We had teachings and meditations every day. No distractions from the outside world, clean and healthy eating, and no alcohol. In this space, I was really able to open my channel pillar to receive clearly about what it was that I needed to do to 'fix' the situation that I had created for myself. I kept hearing the word – surrender. Do you understand how powerful that word is? Take a moment right now to close your eyes and imagine yourself letting go of EVERYTHING and having control over nothing. My ego just could not completely let go. I still wanted solutions to 'fix' my financial mess. It was in a meditation one day that I received that I needed to completely change my focus, in my business and in my life. To truly merge with my divinity in every aspect of my life. Not just because I wanted a solution to fix a problem, but because I was in service to my soul. No longer listening to the advice of the mind that created the situation I was currently in, but instead raising my frequency to sit in a space of service. Service to my soul. Sitting in this frequency requires you to surrender all attachments to outcomes, people, places, etc. And it was then that I received a name – 'Shambala'.

My ego had had a field day with all of this. I was, at this stage, still harnessing the ability to sit in high frequency without allowing my mind to interfere. So my ego decided that this meant I needed to fully restructure my current business and turn it into a holistic healing space in the middle of the city. This meant starting from scratch. But it also meant I would be serving my soul's purpose. I quote from my journal – *This is an opportunity to run a successful business from an open heart, in a spiritual way. I will openly invite the angels and masters through the doors to spread their love and compassion through the floors and walls of the store. I will rebuild the business from a space of love. New staff, new energy, new passion.* Little did I realise that this was exactly what I was about to manifest, but just not in the city.

On returning from Hawaii, I went gangbusters. I had a plan to change the name of the business, our services and even start teaching the body of work that I was just completing, The Masters' Way. I had even signed up to do a crystal healing course and a hot stone massage course to add services to this newly evolving space. This is when things really started to go south. My staff started to turn against me, the clients started to drop away, and the name Shambala that I wanted for my shop was the name of a fancy new day spa right across the road!

I thought I had received it all so clearly, so I was really beginning to doubt myself and soon judgment became my embodiment. Anxiety, panic, fear and such strong attachments to a space that I had not only grown up in but was so reliant on. The space was starting to let me go but I just couldn't see a life without her. She was surrendering me, but I was holding on so tight. The tighter the grip, the bigger the cuts and blisters.

Then, finally, my divinity put something magical in my path. It must have seen that I needed a nudge, or it may have even been divine timing. The little beauty salon down the road from home in the picturesque setting was suddenly available to lease. I didn't even give it a second thought, I just said YES! I was pulsed. I had no money and I was up to my eyeballs in debt but I just needed this space. I knew I could make it work. The rent alone was a tenth of what I was paying in the city. I could create 'Shambala' but it would be in the hills. I could have my self-mastery school and do a few treatments here and there to keep the overheads covered. I could possibly even draw a wage out of this space to keep more cash flow in the city salon. Here was the answer that I needed – two salons! So I borrowed even more money and *bam!* Shambala in the Hills was born.

Little did I know that I was in the process of birthing a whole new life for myself, which as we know, can be an extremely painful and sometimes very slow process. So here I was with not one, but two salons, with two very different flavours. Nothing had shifted financially for me, yet I felt like something had to give. I needed to surrender. I had more to gain from surrendering, and I had a lot more to lose if I held on.

In a mediation one day I was guided very clearly to surrender the city salon and focus on Shambala, so I made a conscious decision to sell the city salon. Again, this surrender was led by my ego. Being attached to an outcome of seeing the legacy of the business live on. Not wanting to be responsible for the demise of a well-established name, and not being able to own the title of failure.

It took six months for the settlement of the business to go through and by this time my debt far outweighed the value of the business. I ended up selling the business for the value of the rent outstanding that I owed, and I didn't see a cent. It didn't even land in my bank account, it went straight to the landlords. I tried to justify to myself that the value I took away from this business was a well-paid job for twelve years, and as a client so superbly put it – "You didn't buy a business, you bought a wage." Yet I still had so much debt.

Shambala in the Hills was a second-hand project. Second-hand furniture, lower cost products and 'basic' everything, compared to the glitz and glamour of the city. It was me slowing down and taking a breath. I never expected it to turn into what it is today, and I would have laughed loudly with tears in my eyes if ten years ago someone had told me my future.

Five years ago, I answered a question in my journal – *What would I like to have/be?* My answer was:

Reduce my financial responsibilities
Run a simple, successful business and stay ahead of my finances
Be a teacher and guide others
Help others through several healing modalities

And I can say that I have manifested this. I have created this. I received it from my divine feminine heart and created it through my divine masculine light. This answer was me receiving guidance from my soul. No attachments to outcome. Pure divine guidance.

I had to, in the end, go bankrupt. Talk about failing to the next level. I was guided by my divinity to do this, and I want to see the stigma of having to choose this option be lifted. I mean, some people are complete arseholes and do take advantage of the system, but I see it as a blessing that we live in a country that provides so many options for people who get caught in the dark and can't find their way home. My worst fear was actually my saviour. There are so many options available for individuals who get stuck. I didn't have to lose my house or car, or surrender Shambala. For some that may be the case but I believe that I lead with my heart open. I made decisions that were uncomfortable and I chose paths that I didn't want to tread. But I emerged on the other side as a beautiful butterfly.

Heart-centred leadership is one that allows growth. It's often uncomfortable, messy and ugly but it puts you on your divine path. On this path, there is grace and ease. On this path, you can hold sacred space for others and lead them to their divine truth. Shambala in the Hills is a true reflection of the energy I am now. It is a beautiful portal of energy that simply holds space for people. It nurtures, it supports and she has been my lady-in-waiting. I'm just so sorry it took me so long to give her the credit she deserves. She is not a second-hand project, she is my heart portal. She is constantly unfolding her petals one by one with each surrendering process. I am not a failure. I am love, I am light, I am divine.

Cherie Melina

Hi there. I am Cherie Melina Anderson. Holistic beauty therapist, mentor, teacher, guide, healer and space holder.

I work from a beautiful space in the Perth Hills, in the suburb of Roleystone, called Shambala in the Hills. I would drive by this space in the past, each time thinking to myself, *I need to be there*. I made it happen, and have been here for the last five wonderful years.

I have been naturally listening and holding space for people in a compassionate, understanding way for twenty-five-plus years, whether that be in one of my beauty salons over the years or in social environments. People have always seemed to gravitate towards me for what I thought to be no specific reason. Through much learning, life lessons included, I can now see that I have always been channelling frequency in one way or another without even realising it.

I decided to embark on a spiritual course called The Masters' Way and later, Opening to Channel, over the space of four years to deepen my sense of self, master my energy and channel my divine nature. I have now come to be a teacher and facilitator of this body of work, coaching groups in this self-mastery programme over the last five years.

Teaching this course and using the practices in my treatments has allowed me to step into serving my soul and sharing my gifts in a way that I couldn't have imagined. I now incorporate crystal healing, channelled guidance and support, mentoring and coaching as well as beauty therapy. I especially love working with those that are beginning their spiritual journey and hungry for knowledge as I remember being that person too.

I have two beautiful kids (sixteen years apart), and a wonderfully supportive partner in life. I love watching my kids becoming their expressions of their souls and gently guiding them, feeling blessed that they picked me to be their mother.

I also feel blessed to have my beautiful work space where I get to meet wonderful people and have amazing opportunities (like this one) to share my gifts and expansion with all that are open to receive.

Website: www.shambalainthehills.com.au
Facebook: www.facebook.com/shambalainthehills
Instagram: www.instagram.com/shambalainthehills

Rachael Bryden

YOUR HEART'S TRUTH

When I was invited to write in this book full of amazing souls, I actually felt blessed to be able to come forward. There are many chapters in our lives and in this chapter I wish to inspire others to realise that we're all worthy of something great in our lifetime.

Have you ever asked yourself … *Who am I?* If so, then who are you? And then who are you deeper than that? And even deeper than that? Ask yourself this on a deeper level each time and see what comes up for you. We're not just labels … Yes, we're mothers, our occupation, sisters, aunts, friends, etc. … But, who are you? I am me. An entity, a gift that changes and moulds and I'm here to help transform the world.

My story and my message begin from within. How I've forever felt that there's a voice inside me, just itching to jump out and shout to the world, "We're here to be awakened and remember who we are!" To feel like I'm at the top of a mountain, sharing my message with it echoing across and through the valleys and creating that ripple effect … the legacy of why I'm here. To find those tools over the years that we need to help us let go of what is holding us back from living our best life and speaking our truth. I feel that's why we're here; to learn how to use the tools we find along the way to help open ourselves up and undo the conditioning of the human learnt behaviours, and to be able to have the human experience at a higher vibration or frequency.

This is how I felt as a young one, not realising my gift and the conditioning on my human experience that was about to slow me down in being able to speak my truth. I longed to share what I could see and feel and for someone to be able to understand and explain it to me, which meant finding my tribe along the way whilst living in a household where I was actually raising my parents as well. I knew that I wanted to be part of transforming the world, but how was I to do this if the souls around me didn't understand my language? One tool that I was taught was how to be healthy and I wanted to take that to a deeper level.

Which leads me to the question … Have you ever felt like you're living two lives? Living one way that serves you and another that serves others? Having something inside you and not knowing how to release it and get it out to the world, or even yet … how to understand it yourself? As a child, I was lost, yet I could feel my difference and unique self. As a teenager, I knew my purpose and my want to transform the world, but I was amidst the chaos of survival. And going into my adulthood, I was a mother who knew what I had to do, all whilst focused on teaching my babies how to be their whole selves. The whole time I was living two lives … Though I do now see it was a challenge that seemed to have helped my kids learn who they could be, in comparison to what didn't resonate with them, as I'd often bring awareness to attributes of those that made them feel uncomfortable and explain how these experiences were guiding them on how not to be.

All of this and my interest in health led me to ask from an early age; *How can I help transform the world, leave my mark, teach from a young age and be noticed?* I so eagerly wanted to take health, fitness, my passions and my spirituality to another level. It seemed to me that people were only working on the physical and what they looked like; they weren't seeing the whole picture. Yet what ten-year-old would be heard on this topic and be taken seriously from an adult's perspective? I wanted to help others balance their body from the inside out. I'm so grateful that not only did I find my outlets in dancing, music, sport and healthy cooking from an early age, but these helped me ground myself and express myself through energy and to release all that was inside.

My dance teacher Sondra McGougan was one of my heroes. They say we all have a hero or someone we look up to between the ages of seven to fourteen as part of our developmental growth in our subconscious, and this gorgeous soul was one of my heroes who'd not only push me through my boundaries and out of my comfort zones, and got me up for early morning starts to practise her personal training on, but who also taught me how to feel through music and trust the person I was. I will always be grateful as I've used those tools throughout my entire life. Sondra taught me about the physical and I embraced all the knowledge that I could about the spiritual using reiki, which as a teeneger by then, I'd found some tools I could use to help guide others and start my journey. Some nights I was at home and on others I lived with someone who is like an older sister to me, Cecily, and all her sisters took me under their wing and helped guide me in my spiritual growth.

It was challenging teaching myself and at the same time being within a schooling system that didn't believe in the way I saw the world. In my senior years of school I felt as though I was being pressured to do tasks that didn't align with me. I never knew there were other options besides TEE (these days known as ATAR). Being a free spirit, I struggled to see through my mothers request that I go to university and become something amazing that she wished for me to be. I hadn't yet realised that I could shinc by being me.

My mother had never fulfilled her own desires as she came to Australia in her senior year (as a ten-pound Pom) and was put back a year at school as most of the English were apparently back then, being told that they weren't smart enough (even though she'd already learnt all that they were being taught). So she decided to leave school to work. I must say that I did resent my mother's desire for me to go to university for a few years because of the pressure of trying to understand English at school myself. And even though I did enjoy human biology, and I did go down the road of studying it more in-depth, I felt that during my senior years at school I was being directed along the wrong path.

Looking back now I've had my own children and in guiding them on their path, I'm grateful for the lessons I did learn throughout my teen years. If my mother hadn't wanted the best for me, I'd not have learnt how to be so strong and determined to shine my own light.

Being stuck at a school I did not want to be at, I had to find something to keep me in my right mind, and seeing the world so differently meant that how I learnt felt incompatible with the system. I had to get through school and master how to learn in order for me to grow and move forward. Luckily I had an amazing human biology teacher, who spent time teaching me how to explain my learnings and understand what she was teaching in the first place through diagrams. I got through my last years of school by drawing these diagrams and explaining them to pass.

But, I felt frustrated within myself because I wasn't speaking my truth. I longed to find a way to get through to the people that weren't seeing the bigger picture. They didn't understand the equation that leads to a healthy lifestyle. It's not just healthy eating so we look good; it has to nourish and balance what we're missing too. Even though I did my dancing, sport and aerobics combined with healthy eating, how could I teach others?

I did some reflecting. Throughout my life, those older friends I've had were my guiding angels and each taught me something that I could use in my chapters along my journey so far. But little did I realise that as they were teaching me what not to do and how to empower myself, they were also leading me towards helping them to find the answers they needed for themselves. You see, perception is projection, and vice versa. I love the universe and how those energies reflect what we're here to learn.

As an older teen, I was the counsellor and listener for relationships of others. They say we meet people that we mirror in order to learn more and understand. This is how the universe teaches us, so each time we can level up and move on to our next chapter. Every soul I've ever met holds a special place in my heart and I'm grateful for the learnings I can share to help others grow and empower their lives.

So it was time for me to finish school and go out into the world and start living my truth. When I left school, I went straight into work and studying. I ended up having to study at a few different academies as the government didn't approve of the funding for natural therapies so the schools got shut down, but nothing was to stop me from doing what my heart and soul were calling for. I studied natural therapies, I qualified in reiki and breathwork, and got a few certificates from TAFE too, before then merging into my adulthood.

Becoming a mother in my early twenties, I'd attracted the kind of relationship that I'd grown up around, and with that being a familiar feeling, I went inwards again, feeling the pull towards living two lives again. I was repeating the same cycle in motherhood that I had lived as a child and teenager, always living one way that served me and another way that served others. As a mother, I lived my heart-centred ways, in a state of peace and flow, respecting my values, beliefs and learning as much as I could whilst my partner was away. And then when he was back, my life was put on hold until he flew out again.

As I delved deeper into my natural therapies and reflexology, which later led to me to further my studies in facial diagnostics and biochemical ways, I found different opportunities and awakenings were happening around me, and just how much I longed to feel free and not trapped so I could truly live my passion. A dear soul said to me, "Where has that fire gone that you had about you?" I didn't realise that over time, being in that relationship had put it out. I had allowed him to manipulate and control me in ways that he couldn't even understand when I'd speak. He didn't believe in what I believed in, nor understood what I studied, which led me to doubt myself in getting clients and knowing my worth. I still believed in what I did and knew my purpose, yet I needed an income as he was a big spender, so I got some local work at a store. Whilst working there, it helped me see that I was able to guide others with the knowledge I had. People would gladly ask for my advice, however they wouldn't book an appointment or consult because they questioned why I was working at the local store and not doing my business. "How can you be a naturopath, biochemist and coach if you work here?" they'd ask.

You see, I believed in my words and what I could do and how it all made a difference. But my subconscious didn't believe I could get the clients. So if you doubt yourself, the universe isn't flowing and people will doubt you too. I felt lost … I was keeping everyone else happy, except myself. I had lost my spark and I was just living for my children, teaching them all I knew and to respect themselves and follow their heart's truth.

I still longed for that freedom, just to be my own free spirit! Free to share with the world what I could see and how we could help ourselves grow by embracing and jumping into the old ways of centuries and bringing them into the now. My biochemistry has allowed me to embrace this old way and teach others how to balance their bodies from the inside out.

I was once told that my message was to bring the old into the new. I love the 1700s and 1800s, and sciences combined can be a beautiful combination. And so it was then that I decided I was aware of what I desired in life; my own values and beliefs. I could see where I was headed and I knew what was holding me back. I knew my purpose on a deeper level now, but how was I going to get my choices to line up with my values? I was still choosing to continue living two lives, which meant my values and beliefs were being anchored a bit longer and my progress to where I desired to be would be a slower journey. Until I woke one morning and just knew; the words came out of my mouth and I could be free. I wasn't going to allow myself to feel trapped, held back or doubt myself anymore.

It's funny how it happens, you just know. What you could be doing with your life just flows through you, and I knew in that moment that I had to fulfill my passion, and the fire inside me began to ignite again! The universe started putting those opportunities in front of me and I said YES to them and felt the anchors being lifted. We're all born with a purpose; it's the journey along the way, the lessons we are faced with and the mistakes we make that help guide us on our path to find it.

My passion to transform the world has always been so powerful on the inside. But sometimes we get lost in the process and the purpose of why we're here and how we can achieve our goals. Whilst dancing between two lives, my calling was always there to bring those old ways into the now that nurture our natural basics. This connection between ourselves and the earth was always so strong, right there alongside the system whose structure and values never resonated with me. We get conditioned from such a young age and we're taught to either follow our path or follow the crowd. Following the masses may get you where you're going, but it will always take you a hell of a lot longer. Instead, follow that fire in your belly – the voice telling you that nothing is holding you back but yourself.

What has inspired me the most on my journey is the value system of how we all grow through different stages of our lives at dissimilar times. Even though people could hear me, they didn't understand me or my language. So how was I going to get my message out into the world in order to make a difference? I'd share what I did with people and the difference we could all make for ourselves, yet growing up in the conditioning of society, others would turn it around so that they'd want to give me guidance – even though I could feel and see what was around me, and my purpose was to help others transform their negative emotions and let go of what was holding *them* back.

That's when I realised that so many of us in this world really do see what we need to do, but we don't want to do it for fear of actually growing and not knowing who we are. It's actually the most amazing process and I'm blessed to be able to share it with souls that do wish to transform and grow, and want to let go of all that is holding them back and what they believe about themselves. The process is beautiful and life-changing. We're here to live! Not just exist! We're here to live our truth, and to not have that endless voice doubting us in what decisions we make. To be true to ourselves and to be achieving our goals, and in turn, we grow together. Really, if we can speak from our heart and not get in our own way, then we're living who we are.

So many people say, "I don't know my purpose." Well, what lights you up? What keeps appearing in front of you at opportunities that you don't engage with and regret later? This is your purpose, your calling, your aha moment that will keep being put in front of you until you say yes. Or they will be your lessons until you learn them. Are you listening to what's around you, or are you listening to who's around you?

I've always questioned if my friends around me are inspiring me; if it's a beautiful circle of growth. We will always encounter those souls in our lives who want us to do what they think is right for us, and this to me, is like being in a cage. I spent a lot of my years allowing others to control me and cage me, and now I'm very aware of it. I walk away and don't entertain the energy or conversation, and also encourage my children to be true to who they are and their decisions on what feels right for them.

So this leads me to share, *What does being heart-centred mean to me?*

For me, it's living a life that is free, not only in oneself but to feel aligned in your heart, mind and soul. It's being true to yourself and speaking your own words of wisdom and sharing your stories. Body, mind and soul are three heartfelt words that stem from a part of my heritage, my history and my past, and they align with my truth, my purpose and where I feel drawn to. The triskele is the Celtic symbol for body, mind and spirit so it resonates beautifully with who I am and how I share my biochemical balancing of the body, neurolinguistic programming (NLP) for the mind and my spiritual self embracing this experience. My business name is Triskele Therapies, and it's allowed me to throw myself into my workshops, allowing the universal flow around me to embrace me in the freedom of sharing my passion, life's purpose and speaking my heart's truth.

I feel there's something more to us than why we're here, a deeper level, even. Like all those beautiful gems that lie under the surface, waiting to be found or freed to shine our light and talents. To have our breakthroughs and share them with the world. Why I'm here is so much bigger than me. As I said before, it's to create that ripple effect and enjoy the awakening of this human experience. To leave our legacy for the future generations.

As they say, "In a world of worriers, be the warrior."

Rachael Bryden

Hi, I'm Rachael Bryden, a holistic healer who loves wide open spaces and embracing my free spirit. My love of natural therapies has been with me since I was a child, from mixing up herbs outside in the dirt to my healthy ways as a teen. I studied in reiki and breathwork during my late teens, which as an adult I incorporated into my passion of biochemistries, in which I completed my Diploma of Biochemistry and Facial Diagnosis. I then went on to do my master practitioner training in NLP, Time Line Therapy® and hypnotherapy. I now combine all these modalities in different ways to complement each other, balancing the body from the inside out.

I am dedicated to supporting beautiful souls in releasing old habits, beliefs and trauma they've been holding onto subconsciously … whether it be from their childhood, past lives or passed down genealogically. I enjoy empowering souls on a physical, emotional and spiritual level and helping them break through their feelings of anything holding them back and ridding those old beliefs to feel whole again. This beautiful rewiring process is an amazing journey and I'm blessed to share this life-changing transformational experience with divine souls and those I'm yet to meet.

I was born seeing auras and have lived a spiritual journey whilst being a country girl at heart, and my love of animals, the hills, the sound of the ocean and waves bring me balance, grounding and inner peace. Living near the Stirling Ranges and all its beauty is something I'm truly grateful for and enjoy each new day as it comes.

Being a mother of two young adults, whom I'm very proud of and appreciate for the lessons that they teach me, has also helped me live my purpose and create that ripple effect with such gratitude and honour for those around me.

Facebook:	www.facebook.com/Triskele-Therapies
	www.facebook.com/rachael.bryden.3
Instagram:	www.instagram.com/rach_inner_health
Email:	rachaelbryden@live.com

Tracey Anne Cecil
STORY OF A HEART-CENTRED LEADER

How did I become a heart-centred leader? As I sit here contemplating where to start, a voice inside my head says, *Just write.* So, I do, as that's what a heart-centred leader does; they listen to that first voice in their head. They listen to their instincts and they are guided by the energy around them. They listen to the reactions they get in their body. They feel their way into every situation, with a knowing. They don't follow strategy or statistics; they follow their heart.

We all start life as heart-centred beings, then life chips away at us bit by bit. Our circumstances, events and experiences determine whether we stay heart centred or not.

I run a very successful heart-centred business and I have learnt to follow my instincts and trust in them. It wasn't always like this. I would self-sabotage because of old hurts and beliefs that I was holding onto. I would not take action and let things slide. I wouldn't put myself out there, I would play small. I didn't think I was deserving of good things.

Trauma has a major effect on how you lead yourself and trust yourself. It can be a major event or a chain of small events that slowly knock you down, and before you know it, you are in a situation where you have lost your power to lead yourself. You have given your power away to someone or something.

Sometimes you have to go right back to the beginning. Looking deep into the shadows of the mind and the cauldron of your emotions and tap back into that innocence of pure knowing and trust.

Let me share with you now the chain of events and learnings that led me back to being a heart-centred leader.

I have always been intuitive and sensitive to the energy around me. Reading people and situations has always been a gift or a curse, depending on how you look at it. Knowing when someone doesn't like you or that they are a fake and a liar is a curse. Especially when everyone else thinks they are wonderful. Knowing that your children or your partner is lying is a blessing. My children still say, "Don't even try to lie to Mum." Knowing that someone is cheating on someone else is a curse, if you are close to both people. Knowing that someone is cheating on you, or your client, is a blessing.

I was always the person that people would come to when they needed help. But this didn't stop at people. Animals would follow me home and spirits thought it was okay to talk to me, showing themselves to me, and if I ignored them, they would poke and prod at me.

I slept with the blankets over my head long into my adulthood. I was a magnet for negative energy that wanted to be transformed into something more positive. I didn't know this back then but I know that now.

I was very open to my gifts of sight and feeling. I acknowledged imaginary friends and I truly believed that I could have whatever I wanted. I would decide I wanted to do something and I expected to manifest these things into my world.

Even when I first started school, I believed in myself and the power of thought so much that I believed the school sport team I was in would win just because I was in it.

I remember in grade prep, the school was having a school ball and they wanted someone to do a solo for the opening of the ball. My mum had enrolled me in dance class, as I really wanted to be a ballerina. I hadn't even done a class yet and guess what? I put my hand up. Yes, me, who had never danced before, put my hand up.

Well, I was enrolled; in my innocent child brain, I did dance. I believed I could and so I did. My mum did, however, have to organise extra private dance lessons, so I looked like I knew what I was doing.

I realise that it was my dancing days that first prompted me to question myself. This was the moment that I realised that life was full of competition and judgement. I was a good dancer. I had been picked for a solo at a school ball, for goodness sake. I danced in front of a full audience, including the Mayor of Footscray.

I was tall for my age, I wasn't a tiny little dot. So this meant I was put in the back row and when we danced in pairs, you guessed it, I was given the boy part. This was bad enough on it's own, but because I was sensitive to energy, I could pick up on what people were thinking. I noticed the nastiness towards me from the other dance mums. Dance mums can be very competitive, wanting their princess to be the best. There were a lot of princesses, so therefore a lot of dance mums. So I started thinking that others were better than me.

I left dancing when I started high school and started spending all of my spare time with horses. My auntie taught me to ride on an old mare called Cream Puff; she was so beautiful, but she only liked two speeds – walk and stop.

I wanted a horse of my own so badly but I had to prove to my parents that I was committed first. I was lucky to be given the opportunity to take care of and ride a young, two-year-old gelding called Sooty. I'm not sure of his breed, he was a bit of this and a bit of that. He was tall and lanky and had a very large head.

The first time I rode him, I ended up in the creek on my arse. He certainly had more than one speed, and you only had to think about going faster as he would feel your energy. I jumped on Sooty and gave him a kick, like I had to with Cream Puff, and well, you get the picture. I learnt very quickly that my energy would affect the performance of the horse. I know now that the energy we put out is what will be returned to us.

I loved taking care of Sooty. Sooty and I volunteered for Riding for the Disabled. I was amazed at how brave and trusting they were, especially the young blind girl I had the pleasure of leading. I learnt a lot from those kids, about strength, courage and determination. I was literally being a heart-centred leader.

Sooty and I joined the local pony club, and this was my next lesson in judgement. I arrived with a borrowed saddle, a borrowed lanky mixed-breed horse with a big head. We really didn't fit into their standards.

I was finally gifted my own horse. I can still feel the gratitude I felt when my parents presented him to me. I had given up hope on having my own horse. I remember having the shits with my parents, as I really wanted a new pair of riding boots and they hadn't bought me them either.

I was really angry. They had gone away for the weekend with my auntie and uncle and forgotten about my boots that I needed for pony club. They arrived home and my auntie asked me to come and help her feed her horses. I remember bitching about the fact that I was never going to get a horse and that I had to go to pony club with old boots. I bitched and grumped while we fed her horses.

My auntie took me into the stables. And there he was. Ratty, my beautiful fifteen-hand bay gelding. He was perfect. That's where my parents had gone. They had bought me my very own horse.

He had a scar on his back leg and that's where he got the name Ratty from. Short for rat shit. He was bred for showing but when he injured his leg after being spooked by the wind and getting caught in a fence, they said he was rat shit for showing. I didn't care, I was so happy to have myself a beautiful fifteen-hand-high, bay thoroughbred-cross-quarter-horse gelding.

The next day I was up early to go ride my new horse Ratty. I went to put the saddle on his back and he jumped around like he was scared of it. I finally got the saddle on and put my foot in the stirrup and up he went. It turned out that he'd had a bad experience with a western saddle where the back girth slipped into his flanks.

I didn't want to upset him so I rode him bareback for a couple of months and we both loved it. I could feel every movement he made. I could ride him without a bit in his mouth and no saddle and we were calm and free and happy. I would come home from school and I would be straight up to the farm. Just me and my horse. No rules, just enjoying each other.

My friend talked me into coming back to the pony club. I had a bad feeling about the pony club, and I should have listened to my instincts. It was a very windy day, and I arrived at pony club riding my new horse bareback. First, I was forced to put a saddle on his back and stay on while he reared. They then looked him all over and told me how he would be no good for showing because of the scar on his leg.

Feeling disheartened, I persevered trying to get on his back. The instructor yelled at me the whole time. I finally got on but he was stressed, and his head hit me in the face as he reared up and my tooth went through my lip.

They made me stay on his back, blood dripping down my chin and dirt blowing into the wound. He had overcome his fear of the saddle but his fear of the wind had heightened and so had mine. Not to mention the hate for pony club.

I started working in stables when I was fifteen and had the pleasure of leading again, teaching beginners to ride horses. I taught them to trust their instincts, trust themselves and trust their horse. It doesn't matter if you have the best gear and the most expensive horse; if you don't lead your horse with compassion, trust and understanding you have nothing. I learnt that horses were affected by their experiences. We need to muck out their negative experiences, just like mucking out the shit from the stable.

It is the same for people. We need to lead ourselves by trusting in our instincts, our intuition and our own thoughts. We need to really listen and trust and heal from our past experiences. Every time I didn't listen to my instincts, my intuitive voice, I was led in the wrong direction or things didn't turn out.

I am a strong believer in the power of thought and law of attraction. Extrasensory perception (ESP) and psychic abilities were normal in our family. I was taught that if you wanted to contact someone, you only had to think about them, and if you wanted something to happen then you could make it happen.

I believed in ghosts and I knew that they were true as I had seen them and felt them. I had an imaginary friend, Henry, that is still with me today. I have many other imaginary friends that I now call my guides.

As a child, I visualised God as a beach ball, with all the colours of the rainbow. I felt the energy around me; I was seeing the colours of the energy of the universe.

It was from being annoyed by stuff that I couldn't see, that led my interest into the unknown. I wanted to know what was annoying me and why I knew things before they happened, or why I knew things about people that I shouldn't know.

As I got older, the annoyance got stronger. I chose to block it out and hide under the covers. I wasn't listening to my instincts, intuition and definitely not to my guides. I was fearful and carrying so much emotional baggage that I couldn't possibly listen to my intuition. My cauldron was full of poison and sludge, and you can't drink from a poisoned cauldron. It blocks your intuition, flow and joy.

I follow the pagan traditions now and proudly call myself a witch. Being a witch is all about working with energy, reshaping it and changing it. I don't fly around on a broom, I don't turn people into toads. I certainly do not worship the devil; I don't even believe in the devil. It is not about power over others.

The word witch comes from the word willow, meaning to bend, as in Wicca. We bend and shape the energy around us to facilitate change in our lives and help facilitate change in other people's lives.

I am now a woman that is connected to nature and its energy, and to my own energy and the energy of the universe. I have tapped into my own inner wisdom. Witch is also often translated to wise one.

By awakening all the elements that reside within us, and understanding how they affect us in the physical, mental, emotional and spiritual realms, we can release and grow with flow. Through circle and ritual, we understand the cycles within ourselves and how the seasons and the moon phases affect us. And how we can use and align with these energies to help us to clear and restore emotions, limiting beliefs and so much more.

There have been many times I thought I should stop using the word witch, but I am reminded by my guides and ancestors that it is my purpose and mission to take back the power for those that were belittled, burnt, drowned, cast aside and given the name witch, just for being heart-centred leaders, midwives, healers, wise women and men. Those that trusted their inner voice, believed in magick, their intuition and led themselves by trusting in themselves.

Following the old Celtic traditions of the craft has brought me great understanding of myself and the energy around me. It has helped me stand in my own power and help others stand in their power. Being a witch has led me into new territory with confidence, and has taught me to lead myself and follow my instincts and to trust in my feelings and intuition.

It has brought me back into my magick, into my childlike sense of wonder. It has taught me to take responsibility for my own life, and it has given me the power of choice. The knowledge to trust. The wisdom to know and be.

When I was young, I believed that I could do anything. I believed that I would grow up, get married, have children and live happily ever after. I believed that the world was a safe place. I soon learnt that life wasn't guaranteed. That it wasn't always safe and that life was cruel sometimes. I learnt that not everyone got to grow up. That people and animals die. That they leave this physical world and they can leave just like that.

The day after my fifth birthday, my grandparents and two uncles were killed in a tragic car accident. This was one of the biggest events that shaped who I was and how I felt about myself. I had no idea how this event would cause self-sabotage in my life. It was a tragic day that I will never forget.

I remember being on the front verandah climbing the wrought-iron banister when the police came to the door. I remember telling them that I had turned five. I was happily and confidently chatting to the police and then I heard my mum screaming and crying.

Mum was never given any therapy for her grief; she was twenty-three years old. My dad was twenty-two and he had to identify their bodies. My mum and dad just shoved their grief away. Mum said she was offered valium but it made her feel numb. She just coped by saying, "I had parents and two brothers and now I don't."

Every year on my birthday, there was always the reminder of the loss of my mum's parents and brothers – my grandparents and uncles. My mum would put on a brave face and give me parties and try to look happy. I always knew that she was sad.

It has only been the last few years that I've realised the guilt I carried around because of this event. I felt guilty celebrating my birthday. I guess a few years of believing this started shaping me on what I thought I deserved. I stopped believing I could have everything I wanted. I lost that innocence of belief in myself.

The seed had been planted in my unconscious mind and it started to grow as I got older. The unconscious parts of ourselves will create events in our lives to prove ourselves right. I was still confident to a certain degree; I was in the popular group at school, I had lots of friends and I loved my horse and my life.

However, I hated high school and I was shit at maths and hated science because of the teachers. I failed year nine and believed I was dumb. If I had spent as much time on maths and my homework, as I did sitting in front of the mirror, practising smoking, my dance moves and thinking about horses and boys, I might have passed. I repeated year nine feeling stupid and dumb; more evidence added to my unconscious.

When I was sixteen, we moved from Melton to Kialla, onto a little farm just out of Shepparton. A new life, new school. I met my best friend's brother when I was nineteen and we were married a week before my twenty-first birthday. I had my first baby girl ten months after our wedding and my second daughter seventeen months after that. We moved to a little country town called Girgarre.

I started up my own fitness class, and was asked to work in the local community centre, working alongside a grief counsellor, working with women with low self-worth due to trauma. Before long I was working in several community centres in the area. I was doing meditation and relaxation after exercise before it became a 'thing'.

My husband was an interstate truck driver and a compulsive liar. In 1992, I became pregnant with my son. My husband was never around and he left us without money or a car. He lost our home, as he didn't pay our mortgage, so I packed up and moved back to Melton to be near my parents, who had moved back there a year or so earlier. I also left my thriving little business behind.

My son was born and things didn't get any better. The marriage ended and I ended up jumping from the frypan into the fire with a man that I was working for, teaching boxercise. He turned out to be very violent. I got pregnant to this man early in our relationship and ended up marrying him. We came home from our two-night honeymoon and that's when he first hit me. He was a very violent man and my self-worth had depleted completely. I didn't recognise myself.

After a very violent night, I finally got the courage to leave. It was because of this man, however, that I found my strength to leave. He told me that I should have a reiki done to fix myself. It was that reiki session that changed my life.

I left him and started healing myself. I was not going to be a victim like the women I used to help. I became a reiki practitioner, massage therapist and counsellor, and I healed myself whole.

I believed in myself again. I then manifested Mark, the love of my life, and we have been married for almost nineteen years.

I went on to study more, to learn more about myself and how I could help others. I added tarot, witchcraft, hypnosis, NLP, coaching and so much more to my skill set. I continually healed myself, so I could lead myself. I rely on my instincts and I send out the energy I want back. I believe I can, so I do.

I now teach others to heal themselves; to connect to their magick and how to tap into the energy and frequencies around them. I trust that the right people will find me. I trust and believe in myself.

If you want to be a heart-centred leader you need to continually heal yourself, by going deep into the shadows, believing in yourself and trusting in that pure innocence of knowing and believing, so you can follow and lead with your heart.

Remember: You are the magick.

Tracey Anne Cecil

Hi, my name is Tracey Anne Cecil. High priestess of Celtic magick, Commonwealth-registered celebrant, reiki master/teacher, hypnotherapist, psychic, clairvoyant, tarot reader/ teacher, counsellor, coach and mentor and now, author.

I love everything esoteric and have been dabbling in the magickal arts since I was very young. When I was two years old, I met my imaginary friend Henry, who is still one of my guides today.

We all have spirit guides to help us and lead us on our path. They will communicate with us in different ways and are here to help for many different reasons. We all have a master guide that stays with us from birth to death. Henry is my master guide. I have many others for specific things in my life. They can come and go depending on the energy I need at the time. They may be a god, goddess, angel or a spirit from a past life or ancestor.

I was poked and prodded so much as a kid by things that weren't of this world, that I slept with the blankets over my head well into my adult years. I didn't realise then that they were trying to lead me or ask for my help.

There was the lady who swept the floor at the end of my bed that no-one else could see and the lady who would shake her head at me that freaked me out. My brother still shakes his head slowly with a creepy smile on his face, just to freak me out. I was certain that I was in trouble and she was ticking me off.

My intuition was always strong, and it was only when I ignored my intuition that I found myself in trouble. When I ignored my intuition, that's when I would be poked and prodded.

My interest to learn about these encounters led me to do the work I do today. I now listen to my inner voice and don't just shove things in the cauldron and allow them to brew, boil and bubble.

I am often referred to as Zelda the HypKnoWitch. Zelda's Cauldron is my business, a mixed pot of services to help others grow and flow and unlock their magick. Zelda is my craft name. She is my muse, the keeper of my unconscious/shadow and my magick.

I have been in the healing industry for over thirty years, starting out as a fitness instructor. This led me to working alongside a grief counsellor helping women who had very low self-worth, caused by trauma and grief.

After two failed marriages myself, one being very violent, I was on a mission to not become a victim like those women. I started studying healing modalities and this was my turning point. My mission was then to empower as many women as I could.

Massage, reiki, counselling and then while doing a course on tarot, I found the Way of the Wise. The Way of the Wise is the Way of the Witch, following the old traditions of the Celtic craft. I worked at the place I studied as a tarot reader for several years. I then became a high priestess and then went on to teach the Celtic craft myself.

In 2014 I opened Zelda's Cauldron in a little country town called Trentham. Trentham is in regional Victoria in the shire of Hepburn. I now live in Melton, Victoria; I am a bit of a gypsy and don't like staying in one place too long, but Zelda's Cauldron is now with me wherever I live or go.

I added hypnotherapy and coaching to my services in 2018, and have done many other healing workshops, learning retreats and I will continue to do so. I believe you never stop learning and growing.

In 2020, while in lockdown in Melbourne, I studied to become a celebrant and became a registered marriage celebrant in February 2021.

I am now married to a beautiful man. We have been married for eighteen years and we have six children between us. I have three daughters and one son. I am blessed to also have six beautiful grandchildren.

I am grateful that I get to help others step into their power, their magick and grow with flow every day now. I look forward to connecting with you.

Website: www.traceyannececil.com
Facebook: www.facebook.com/zeldascauldron
                   www.facebook.com/traceyannececil
Instagram: www.instagram.com/zeldascauldron
                   www.instagram.com/traceyannececil
Email: tracey.cecil@live.com.au

Jenny Stanley-Matthews
THE POWER OF BELIEF

"The head will never truly be motivated until the heart knows WHY it should."
– Jenny Stanley-Matthews

What does it mean to be a heart-centred leader? I believe a heart-centred leader is someone who has achieved a level of consciousness where they have become personally accountable for their actions, are aware of their impact on the world and instinctively know that they are a part of a whole.

Experience has shown me that heart-centred leaders are often created early in life and may not realise their potential until they are older and have endured much soul-searching after many lessons learnt. They will have discovered the duality that exists within life; the good, the bad, the light and darkness, and how each exists within each other. Mostly, they will have discovered that challenges can break you or become your biggest teacher and fuel your progress in life.

The duality of life became obvious to me from a very young age. I had a father who I absolutely adored; he was the life of the party, charming, intelligent and could play many musical instruments. He worked as an entertainer, a singer and lead guitarist in a band for all of my youth. He also had another side. He was a functioning alcoholic, mentally abusive, had an explosive temper and had at least one affair that I know of. I know this because she started turning up to the house and eventually moved into our home creating a polygamous relationship where my father had two partners, one being my mother. Us three kids, and eventually my sister who was born from this union, just had to accept that this was our new normal, without explanation. Polygamous relationships usually have the consent of all parties involved, however, I do not believe my mother had much of a say in it and us kids just had to do what we were told. However, the relationships did endure and continued until my father's death at age seventy-eight.

The dynamics of power within relationships became very apparent to me. My mother was an immigrant from Holland, was the eldest daughter from a family of eleven children, had low self-worth and was sixteen years younger than my father. He was the 'king of the castle', and we were always told, "Don't tell your father," as we tiptoed around, enabling his dysfunctional behaviour to continue.

There was also a lot of secrecy, and I became the keeper of secrets. I would keep secret my family dynamics because I did not want to be forced to explain something I did not understand. I would have to pretend that I did not find my father's stash of alcohol in the boat or that when he took us to the park, he would consume a bottle of port before driving us home. I would have to keep secret the torment and mental abuse. And to avoid more ridicule and torment at school, I would eventually have to keep secret the skin condition I developed all over my body. I must admit, I still feel a twinge of guilt divulging this information in this chapter.

This was probably where my interest in empowering people came from, because along with my passion for authenticity, truth and personal accountability, I could see that if my mother felt strong enough to step up (which I know would have been hard with two kids under three years old and pregnant with her third), then my father would have had to become accountable, and everyone's life may have improved.

By the age of five years old, I had developed sores all over my body, which I now know as a kinesiologist, would have been linked to emotional stress. They were excruciatingly itchy and uncomfortable, and there was not a patch on my body that was not covered with them. I would be taken to the children's hospital every three weeks to be examined with the threat of cutting one off to investigate them, which would also put me in a constant state of stress. I had to apply ointments and take tablets that even my mother did not know what they contained. The doctor could not determine what was causing them, only that they were not contagious (and in those days they did not consider the link between emotional and physical conditions).

This would continue for many years and had an impact on my self-image and self-worth. I was an outwardly confident child but very self-conscious on the inside. I always made sure my legs were covered and the other kids could not see my sores.

I learnt a lot about human nature during that time, particularly when a group of older kids gathered around to tease me and chant abuse. I learnt that my response influenced the mob's reaction, and by not showing fear and not letting them steal my energy, they would get bored and leave (I might have learnt this from my father as well). At the same time, I saw a friend of mine crying with compassion (or fear), and again I noticed the duality within a situation.

What I learnt most during this time, and what I believe has led me to be the heart-centred leader that I am today, is the power of the mind. When I was eleven years old, and after enduring this skin condition for nearly seven years, I heard someone say something one day. They said, "Diseases run in seven-year cycles and if you can get rid of the disease within that seven-year cycle, it will not continue." I do not even remember who said it, or whether it was true or why, as an eleven-year-old, I was listening in, but it gave me hope! I had hope of being normal, of being able to sit with my friends and show my skin, of being free of the constant torturing itch, potions and gagging on tablets!

I believed this statement with every ounce of my life force – I had to. I did everything within my power to make it true. I had six months before the end of the seven-year cycle to rid myself of these sores. I resisted scratching them, I ate brussels sprouts because I was told they were good for the skin, I visualised myself sitting with my friends and having smooth legs and arms, and I believed it.

It was three weeks before the end of the seven-year cycle and I had one large sore left on my right leg. My belief did not waiver, and with just days to go, that disappeared as well! I had done it! My belief in my ability to heal or achieve anything that I set my mind to was off the Richter scale. I still have the scar on my right leg today and it reminds me of the power of my mind and my body's healing intelligence.

I believe that earth is a big school, and we are all here to learn. The people in our lives all play a part in that learning as we do in their lives. Sometimes those events and challenges can bring us to the brink and the people who we believe should love us the most treat us badly. As I said, we are all here to learn and when you know better, you do better, and my relationship with my father improved dramatically before his death. My father gifted me his vulnerability as he confessed to me his fear of dying during his last two years of enduring a rare form of cancer. We shared in many discussions, and we shared in his relief when he was given the 'all clear' of his cancer before dying two weeks later of a heart attack. Life has its twists and turns, and every experience has something to teach us. My parents did the best with what they knew at the time and were an accumulation of their own life experiences. I would not be who I am today and have the knowledge and wisdom I have accumulated without them, and I thank them for that.

After leaving school and working in the corporate world as a business analyst for ten years, I married, moved from Sydney to the Hunter Valley and had my daughter. These pivotal life events tend to bring up unfinished business and I started looking for meaning again and reconnected with my intuitive side by studying ThetaHealing®. I have always been quite intuitive and with this knowledge I became particularly good at reading energy, locating injury/illness by doing body scans and remote healings. I still include many of these techniques with my clients today, however, I did not want the responsibility that came with the body scans at the time and stopped practicing that treatment.

It was around this time that I was introduced to kinesiology. Neurolinguistic kinesiology has six levels to learn, and I was told that I could just learn level one and use it to optimise the health and wellbeing of my family, as I now had two daughters and a son. I thought this sounded like a great idea, and the rest is history! Not only did I continue to complete all six levels, but I also completed Touch for Health and a year of physiology and anatomy, becoming an accredited kinesiologist alongside being a full-time mother.

In 2006, with a ten-, seven- and four-year-old, and my husband working twelve-hour days, I launched my business The Centre for Clarity and started seeing clients at home. In 2008, I also started contracting to a five-star health retreat in the Hunter Valley.

During the next ten years of contracting at the health retreat and seeing clients at home, I gained a wealth of knowledge and experience and treated a broad range of clients including celebrities, elite athletes, business owners and some of the wealthiest and most 'successful' people within Australia and throughout the world. I provided treatment for many different issues from terminal illness to relationship issues, and what I found most surprising was the amount of people I saw with self-worth issues. We are taught that money + success = happiness, however, my clients were wealthy, successful and outwardly confident, and they were still not happy. It became obvious that self-worth issues did not discriminate, and I would even go so far as to say that low self-worth can drive someone to become successful to prove something to themselves and others. The problem with this is that the source of power they have created is external to them and when it is external, it never feels secure, continually needing to be maintained and ultimately that person becomes reliant on it, e.g. a slave to their job, or a people pleaser.

This led me to publishing my first book *Embrace Your Power Workbook and Journal* in 2017. I wanted to let people know that they currently possess all the tools and resources within their mind and body to create self-worth, and that they just needed to learn how to use these abilities to their advantage. After seeing such a range of people with self-worth issues, I realised that creating self-worth could not be a one-size-fits-all approach. My workbook introduces the reader to complex ideas in a simple and fun way and includes activities to allow the reader to find their own insight and create a personalised self-worth routine specific to their needs.

Publishing *Embrace Your Power Workbook and Journal* allowed me to reach more people, particularly people who were new to self-development and the power of your mindset. They say that when you positively influence one person it has a ripple effect that impacts 70,000 lives and this idea fuels my passion. I am so passionate about helping people find their power, whether it is seeing a client one on one or through running workshops, because I know that I will not only be improving their life but also the lives of the people around them, and the people around them, and so on.

As I mentioned earlier, my experience in my youth taught me a little bit about human nature, however, when I started learning and practicing this work, it taught me about myself. I believe, to be a heart-centred leader and help others improve their life, you need to do the work on yourself and improve your own life as well. Once I started to tap into some secrets on how the mind works, the body's healing intelligence, how to become personally empowered and much more, it opened a whole new world to me.

I am continually upskilling, adding to my knowledge and improving myself. I am now a qualified counsellor, master hypnotherapist, master life coach, master NLP practitioner, art therapist, international Delete Reset practitioner, international Timeline Reset practitioner, international master Family Freedom Protocol practitioner, and many more powerful treatments.

Clients seek me out because I 'get' them. I combine my life experience and wisdom with my intuitive abilities, along with my accumulation of knowledge, to personalise their treatments. I believe this is what distinguishes heart-centred leaders from other practitioners – we *see* our clients, I mean we really *see* them. Their hearts, their insecurities, their fears, their patterns of behaviours and dependencies, and most of all, their potential because I have never given a client a treatment that I have not experienced myself. I hold space for their energy in a safe, congruent, non-judgemental environment and help guide them until they see their own potential. I have been privileged to guide and witness so many positive transformations over the past fifteen years and teach my clients to be autonomous within their own healing. My job is done when my clients no longer need me and come back every now and then for a bit of maintenance.

If I were to hand over some pearls of wisdom to other aspiring heart-centred leaders about what I have learnt along the way, it would be to know yourself first – the good, the bad and the ugly – and be personally accountable for your own healing before you expect your clients to be.

As a practitioner who comes from a heart space, I often attract clients who resonate with my energy. They may have emotions and/or issues that I can relate to where I have experienced something similar in my own life. Early on in my practice, I found that I was getting caught up in the emotions of my clients and becoming too empathic. I was coming home feeling drained and even became very unwell at one stage when a hernia operation would not heal. I still had a sense of obligation and bandaged up my stomach and dragged myself to work, putting my client's needs before my own.

I learnt the hard way and I know now that you cannot give from an empty cup. You need to prioritise your own health to be able to provide the best treatments to your clients. I learnt to not give myself permission to be in my client's emotional state. You can never know what someone else is feeling, only how you believe they are feeling based on your own experience. Your truth/perceptions/emotions are an accumulation of your specific life experience and so is your clients'.

When I was taking on too much responsibility for my clients and getting caught up in their emotion, I was not adding as much value as I could have been and could have potentially blocked my clients' healing further. Staying objective, holding space, and allowing my clients to go through and express what they needed to, not only preserved my own energy but helped my clients to move forward and away from feeling stuck.

In my experience, many practitioners that come from a heart space tend to find it challenging to ask for money or charge what they are worth, and I was like this for many years. I am passionate about improving people's lives and helping as many people as I can. For me, this created a guilt around receiving and often attracted clients who were not ready to do what was required to improve their life.

Money is an energy. For things to be in balance, there needs to be an equal exchange of energy. When you do not receive payment for services rendered, you have inadvertently given that person an energetic debt to you even though you thought you were being generous. I have now learnt to ask for and accept my value, and I know that the more money I am making, the more people I am helping.

Another big lesson for me was to not take things personally when a client is not improving. When I first started providing kinesiology at a five-star health retreat, the clients were predominantly wealthy people who tended to throw money at you to 'fix' their problem. Unfortunately for them, all the money in the world cannot 'fix' emotional issues without personal accountability. I very rarely see this now, if at all, as I am attracting clients who are ready to do the work. I always give my client the best treatment possible and offer them the opportunity and the tools to release their issues and move forward. If they choose to stay stuck, this is their choice and they have come to me without being ready to heal.

When I see a client for the first time, I now talk about personal account-ability and both of our roles in their treatment. My intention is for all my clients to be autonomous in their healing journey by the end of our treatments and this will never happen if I take responsibility for their healing. My advice to you would be to have certainty that you are giving your best, teach personal accountability in your initial treatments and you will find that you will start attracting clients that are ready to do the work.

As a heart-centred leader, I believe my purpose is to raise the energy/consciousness of the collective, and to do this I need to reach as many people as I can. It is one thing to be passionate about what you do and come from a heart space, but it is another thing altogether to move with the times and have the technical know-how to reach the masses. I was definitely out of my comfort zone when it came to social media and pro-moting myself. I had come from a place of feeling self-conscious about the way I looked and not drawing any attention to myself. I have not only had to learn about social media and technology, but how to love and accept myself before I could put myself out there and expect others to as well. I have definitely been in my growth zone and have learnt how to run workshops, present at public speaking events, post live videos, market myself, and provide treatments and workshops online.

One of the most important things on my journey to becoming a heart-centred leader was to remember that I did not have to do this alone. I have been a part of so many tribes along the way depending on my stage of life. I am still in contact with many of these people today along with new tribes that I have joined. We share our experiences and expertise, raise each other up and support each other along the way. I recommend you find your tribe and connect with other heart-centred leaders because you do not have to be alone on this journey.

I want to finish by talking about what heart-centred means to me, and in doing so, I want to firstly talk about the heart, heart intelligence and heart coherence. The HeartMath Institute has been pioneering research on heart intelligence and heart coherence. They define heart intelligence as a 'flow of intuitive awareness' as the heart has been known to be a major player in our intuition. Heart coherence is when the heart guides the body and the mind, allowing great things to be achieved. Your heart sits in the centre of your being and is highly intelligent, in fact, there is more information being transmitted from your heart to your brain than the other way around so we all naturally think with our hearts.

A coherent heart is believed to create better physical and emotional health, and help you live a happier and more harmonious life. I believe a heart-centred leader has gained a level of coherence within their heart and their life and is able to draw on this energy to help others whether it be their loved ones, peers and/or clients. It is not something that just applies in a business environment – it applies to every aspect of your life.

It is my belief that heart-centred leaders have an innate knowing that we are all connected and when we help another to raise their vibration, we all benefit. Heart-centred leaders are pioneers in delivering this message in our own unique way and helping others gain this awareness to heal, grow and reach their potential.

If you are ready to step into heart-centred leadership, I welcome you and wish you success, happiness, balance and prosperity from my heart to yours.

Jenny Stanley-Matthews

Hi, I'm Jenny Stanley-Matthews and I'm passionate about empowering you to live your best life, and in doing so, also improve the lives of the people around you. I'm excited and determined to be a part of a movement that raises collective consciousness and helps people remember that we are all stronger working together. I have been accumulating my knowledge and wisdom over my lifetime (and probably many lifetimes before), and transmuting my challenges into the fuel that drives me to serve my purpose.

Although I am a very artistic and creative person, my career path started in the corporate world as a business analyst for over ten years before relocating to Regional NSW, Australia, where I married my husband. I then started in my greatest role, eventually becoming a mother to three children – two girls and a boy.

In 2006, after becoming a kinesiologist, and still a full-time mother, I founded The Centre for Clarity and saw clients at my home clinic as well as providing kinesiology to health retreats within the NSW Hunter Valley Region.

In 2017, after seeing many clients struggling with self-worth issues, I published my first book *Embrace Your Power Workbook and Journal*. This was followed by many public speaking events and workshop presentations throughout Sydney, Central Coast (NSW) and Newcastle.

Over the past fifteen years I have been a sponge for knowledge and continually expanding my skills, experience, wisdom, and intuitive abilities to connect with a broad client base. I'm a neurolinguistic kinesiologist, counsellor, master hypnotherapist, art therapist, master life coach, master NLP and Time Line practitioner, author, international Delete Reset practitioner, international Timeline Reset coach, international master Family Freedom Protocol practitioner as well as many other energy and intuitive healing modalities, as I am a very intuitive person.

Being the best mother for my kids has always been my priority and I am proud to say that they have grown to be beautiful, intelligent, caring humans that are already having a positive impact on the world. As my kids became more independent, my practice has also grown to provide online treatments and workshops to international and remote clients. I'm also loving creating and facilitating transformational workshops for retreats, companies and organisations, and being able to reach more people in fun and exciting ways. I still provide treatments at my home clinic as I believe it keeps me relevant and it makes my heart sing to see the positive transformations firsthand in my client's lives.

My intention is not to impress you with what I know, but to enlighten you with how much YOU know and enable you to realise your potential. I want you to discover all the tools and resources you have within you right now to positively transform your life. Whether you are seeing me at a workshop or during a private treatment, I will guide you in my own unique loving way which is fun and empowering and gives you lots of aha moments. I will safely hold space for you while you release the energy blockages and negative emotions that are holding you back, help you shift your mindset and teach you how to 'tweak' those tools and resources and positively transform your life. I know you can do it; you've got this, and I've got you!

Jenny xx

Jenny Stanley-Matthews – The Centre for Clarity
Website: www.jennystanleymatthews.com.au
Facebook: www.facebook.com/centre4clarity
Instagram: www.instagram.com/jennystanleymatthews/
Email: jennystanleymatthews@gmail.com
YouTube: www.youtube.com/channel/UCxsMbWRpU5H7jVbTuGw1E3w

Conny Wladkowski

FROM SURVIVING TO SHINING

Thinking back to the start of my high school years, I struggled. I remember attending a new school where I didn't know anyone and wasn't welcomed with open arms, and after many months of still not being accepted by my peers, I started feeling lonely and sad. I had no friends, no confidence and on top of that, I hated the way that I looked. I didn't fit in anywhere; there was no place for me. Besides going to school every day, which I didn't like, I did nothing else. Friendless and alone most afternoons, I would hide in my room either secretly crying or reading, often wondering why I was even here on this earth.

This was a well-kept secret for many months, even from my parents. They were busy coping with their own issues, so I didn't want to burden them with my struggles, and although they were always there for me, I didn't want to look like a failure. As long as I pretended to be happy, I didn't have to expose my true emotions. After a while my parents realised something was up and did everything to help me, but they just couldn't replace having friends. No matter how often my mum convinced me that I was beautiful and likeable, there was not one inch of my body that believed her. I admired all of the other girls and I longed to look and be like them, craving to be seen and to be liked. But instead, I totally withdrew myself from any kind of social life and absorbed myself in books about reiki and crystals. This is when my intrigue for alternative healing methods developed. At the age of fifteen, an age where most other teenagers were hanging out with their friends partying, I was attending my first ever reiki workshop.

Prior to that my mum had just been diagnosed with MS and I was going to try anything to help her so that she wouldn't end up in a wheelchair, yet I had no idea how I was going to be able to do that. My whole world was crumbling into pieces. My home, my family, my place of comfort and safety, the only thing that was good in my life was about to collapse and I thought it was my job to hold these pieces together. I remember thinking to myself, *I just have to try everything possible*. I just wasn't ready to accept and believe that my mum's condition was incurable, and that it was impossible for her to be healthy and healed.

This is the point when I decided that in my life and in my world, nothing would ever be impossible. This decision created an intense drive within me to prove just that; that nothing is impossible if you decide to fight for it. This was also the time that I developed a dream that one day I would be able to help people heal. I may have deviated off that track a couple of times over the course of my life, but I never once lost the path and deep down inside I always believed that this dream would come true one day and that this is what I was here for.

In the years that followed, I engaged in many different modalities from energy healing, to mindset work and kinesiology. Although I discovered these amazing modalities and soaked up all the information like a sponge, sitting up night after night reading, it was still just a hobby for me. I performed sessions on a friend, on my parents and used it on myself, but I hadn't considered doing it as a job just yet. Whilst I was already full of knowledge and tools, I wasn't quite satisfied yet. It wasn't enough for me to go out and share this knowledge with people. I just hadn't found that one thing for me that swept me off my feet; that thing that would become the game changer and create an experience that changed my life. I was still hunting, searching for something. I was hungry for more. I just knew that there was more out there, I just didn't know what and where to find it.

For sure I was held back by tonnes of limiting beliefs, but still, I wasn't even aware of that yet – it wasn't yet 'a thing'. So I just did what I had to do, and what was kind of expected from me at the time. I did what every Austrian does after high school and I went to university to study something. Without much thought after high school, following in the footsteps of my father, I started studying law. I wasn't happy and I definitely wasn't fulfilled, and although I had absolutely no passion for law, I just powered through and did what I had to do to finish my law degree so I wouldn't disappoint my parents.

Towards the end of my degree, I fell in love with an amazing man, who is still by my side today. I ended up following my heart and moving to Australia, and funnily enough, I couldn't even use my law degree in Australia, which honestly suited me just fine. I started working in my partner's family business, and in my spare time, I devoted myself fully to my fascination and kept on learning more about different holistic healing methods. It was so amazing; living on a completely different continent, exploring new things that weren't yet available in Austria. I was motivated again and excited about life and what else was out there. It had reignited my childhood dream.

At the age of twenty-five, I encountered a serious health issue which turned my world upside down. After multiple surgeries and treatment, my body healed and recovered, but mentally I hadn't recovered from what had been a scary and challenging time. I started feeling anxious and the constant worrying quickly turned into panic attacks. Life was just a struggle for me. Here I was, despite having all this amazing knowledge, just surviving and getting by day by day. I felt like a failure, misunderstood and hopeless. I felt like I had tried everything, but nothing had worked, and I was stuck in feeling anxious and drained.

This was not how I wanted to live. I wanted to enjoy my life, I wanted to enjoy my daughter growing up and enjoy my little family. I wanted to be a great role model for my daughter, be confident and successful and I wanted to be present. But most of all, I wanted to thrive in life and not just survive. I had gotten to the point where everything had crashed and I just couldn't live like that anymore.

It was just after Christmas and we were on a family vacation. We were strolling along the beach, and while my partner and my daughter played and were laughing and enjoying themselves, I was an absolute mess. Here I was on holiday with my beautiful family in the beautiful sunshine, relaxing on the beach in my favourite place, looking out at the ocean and all I could do was cry and shut down to the joy that my family was having – all because of the anxiety. The whole holiday I was riddled with anxious thoughts and struggled daily with panic attacks. When I observed my family laughing and having fun, that was the moment that I knew that I had to do something. I couldn't enjoy my daughter and I wasn't able to enjoy this precious time with my family that we had worked so hard for, to create beautiful and long lasting memories.

That was the moment that I decided to explore something totally new, something totally different. This was my last resort. I didn't want my daughter to be affected by my struggles. I started reading and learning about the power of the mind and tried hypnotherapy, and it totally changed my life. Within weeks I started feeling better and calmer, and things started to shift. I started enjoying life again and I started being more present. It was mind-blowing that something that was such a huge problem and struggle for me – something so difficult and debilitating in my life – was solved within such a short period of time. This was IT. This was the thing that blew my mind. This was what I had been looking for all those years. Yet even still, I wasn't quite yet ready to give up my secure job and jump into being a hypnotherapist.

A few months later, in September 2018, everything changed. My darkest hour and my biggest challenge changed my whole life forever. Little did I know that this was going to be the start of a crazy ride that would finally lead me to living my purpose and fulfilling my dream. At the end of July 2018, I travelled with my family to Austria to spend time with my parents, family and friends again. Full of excitement about this trip, we jumped on a plane. What was meant to be an amazing summer, creating beautiful memories, turned into a nightmare and one of the hardest times in my life.

Shortly after we arrived, my dad started feeling a little bit tired and unwell. We were assured that he just had a viral infection and so we didn't worry too much. I wish we would have known the real severity of his condition. Within two weeks he was in a coma and fighting for his life. I couldn't grasp how a person that was so healthy and full of energy from one day to another could be so sick that he would have to cling onto life. The next three weeks were the hardest time of my life. Every day was a roller-coaster. Moments of hope and believing that he would be fine were shattered by more bad news every day. Desperation and disbelief ripped through my heart.

Every time the phone rang my heart stopped and the fear amplified that this could be 'the phone call'. I stood by his bed every day while he was in a coma talking to him, stroking his hand and begging him to come back. I prayed that he would at least open his eyes one last time so that I could have a chat with him. There were so many things I wanted to tell him. So many more things I wanted to get off my chest and off my heart. I truly believe that he felt us by his side and he fought until the very last minute.

After three weeks he lost his battle, and with my mum by his side, he took his last breath. It crushed me that I never said my final goodbye and gave him a final hug whilst he was still conscious. I couldn't believe it – I was in shock, maybe even in denial. It almost felt like I was watching my life on a movie screen, that it wasn't happening to me. I couldn't grasp that he was gone. It broke my heart even more that my daughter would ask me daily when Opa (Grandpa in German) would be coming home from the hospital.

I always assumed that I had so many more years with him. I pictured so many more moments with him and what an amazing grandfather he would be. Our relationship was very deep and special and we had gotten even closer over the last few years. He was always my go-to person that I would call on for advice. His amazing energy and aura always calmed me and enveloped me with safety. He was my biggest fan and my biggest supporter. I felt like I had lost the ground under my feet. I remained in Austria for another month for the funeral and supported my mum through this difficult time. My brain and body ran on auto pilot-doing whatever I had to do, merely functioning more than anything else.

When I returned back to Australia about six weeks after he had passed away, I plummeted into a big hole. Reality kicked in. I struggled the most in the mornings, and the pain intensified as time went on. Every morning when I woke up, there was always this brief moment, still a bit disorientated and in a daze, where I felt like for a moment that everything was okay and then reality would kick in. Everything happened so quickly; my parents were just starting to enjoy their retirement travelling, and within a few weeks it was all gone.

This is when I realised that I didn't want to waste any more time in my life. Life is so precious and nobody knows when it will come to an end. I developed this driving force within me that I wanted something positive to come out of this experience. I needed to grip onto something that would stop me from falling deeper; something that had a meaning. So I decided to finally live my purpose and become a hypnotherapist. In my free time and on the weekends I studied and learned everything about hypnotherapy. I surrounded myself with everything about the power of the subconscious mind, I signed up for courses, watched videos and read books. I was obsessed, in a positive way, to learn and understand it so that I could finally live my dream and help people.

The more I learned about the subconscious mind and limiting beliefs, the more I realised that there was more work I had to do on healing myself first. I did my own inner child work and worked on my own subconscious patterns that began in my childhood and all of this has led me to the way that I work with clients as a hypnotherapist today.

One of the things that drives me in my work today is that I'm sick of seeing people suffering because of their childhood all their life, and not knowing how to heal from it and who to turn to. We don't have to relive our trauma in order to heal it. This is my mission and my purpose in creating a safe space, with no judgement, with love and holding, so that healing can take place. I'm creating a place of understanding in my work, because I have gone through these things myself. One of the ways I have done this is by combining everything that I have experienced myself through my trauma and my own healing journey with everything that I have learned, and created my own process called The Shine Your Inner Child Process; a process where you can heal without having to go back and relive it.

Inner child work is such an important part to heal yourself. It doesn't matter if you have experienced something traumatic or not in your childhood.

At such a young age we have no critical factor, which is the security guard between the conscious and the subconscious mind. There is no security guard that accepts or rejects suggestions going into our subconscious mind. So anything we see, feel, hear and experience manifests really deeply into our subconscious mind. In our adulthood we act and react based on our experiences in our childhood. Most of our limiting beliefs are formed at a young age and influence the way we view the world today. Nothing 'traumatic' needs to happen to create limiting beliefs. Whether you had the most amazing upbringing or experienced terrible trauma, you will have formed beliefs.

I often have clients that are really confused, because they had an amazing upbringing but they still feel held back. Something that we wouldn't label as a traumatic experience is traumatic enough for a little child to create a limiting belief. This could be when a younger sibling is born and that little person now has to share the attention of their parents, or when the little child hears their parents argue. These are all everyday situations. These everyday situations are enough for a child to create limiting beliefs such as *I'm not loved', 'I'm not good enough* or, *I'm not being heard*, etc. We then go through adulthood not wanting to act and react in a certain way, repeating the same patterns and sabotage behaviours over and over again, however it can feel like we have no control over it. This is why inner child work is so powerful and so important, so that people can break out of repeating the same patterns.

There are also many people who have experienced trauma in their childhood, and are being held back because of it. Abuse in childhood is so common, but still such an unspoken topic and often a taboo subject. So many people suffer their whole life because of it. It usually affects them in all areas of their life but they still don't do anything about it. Many times they haven't spoken about it to anyone. There is often so much shame, guilt, blame and confusion that people carry it as a life-long secret. People are often too scared to go there because they think that they'll need to revisit the trauma. I totally understand where they are coming from.

I find it can be very traumatising and damaging if a client has to go back and relive the abuse or the traumatic event. Our subconscious mind wants to keep us safe so if we don't remember certain details of the traumatic event, there is a reason for it. Also, a lot of the time, people don't even know what the event was or why they are feeling a certain way. The great news is that there is no need to go back and relive the trauma so that you can heal from it. Our inner child hasn't left us – it is still part of us.

What's important is; where are you stuck now, where are you being held back now, and how can we bring you and your inner child into alignment so that you can move forward into a future that you deserve? The story of your past is the story of the past – we cannot go back and change it.

If you keep on focusing on that story over and over again, if you talk about it over and over again, all you do is give it more energy. Energy flows where attention goes. If we put our attention to the solution on how we would rather feel instead, we will create more of that.

I'm hoping to inspire people to start healing before they reach rock bottom. Before it results in diseases, addiction, loss of job, loss of relationship or loss of self. Humans tend to only do something about their situation when they hit rock bottom. Sometimes they are already having to deal with huge consequences, but we don't need to wait until it gets to that point.

Most people think that they can just pretend that nothing has happened and pretend to be fine. I did the exact same thing. For many years I told myself that the experiences weren't affecting me. I had so many amazing reasons that would also back up that theory. I have a university degree. I have a beautiful daughter. I have a full-time job and an amazing partner. I have great friends and I'm really close with my family. I had convinced myself for many, many years that it wasn't affecting me until it all came to the surface. First it emerged bit by bit and I still kept on pretending, and then I got really sick. I faced a very serious health issue and was suffering from panic attacks for many years. This is when I hit rock bottom and simply couldn't push it down anymore. I wish I would have resolved it before it affected my health, because the ripple effect it all had was massive. It is so important to understand that unresolved trauma is affecting us even though we often don't realise it or want to admit it.

Yes, we can put the trauma or the experience in a box and shove that box into the back corner of the house. Our subconscious mind wants to keep us safe and that's why we are able to put it in a box so that we can go on with our life. But one day that box will begin to re-emerge and you'll be suddenly confronted with memories, dreams and emotions of that past trauma. This sudden re-emerging of those emotions and memories doesn't mean that things are getting worse; it actually means that the person is able to deal with it now. It's usually a sign that a person now has the strength and the resources to successfully deal with the emotions.

Alongside my experiences and path to becoming a hypnotherapist, I've learnt so much over the course of my journey about what it means to be a heart-centred leader and succeed in this work. Here are my three tips to ultimate success:

1: CONSISTENCY IS THE KEY

One of the biggest challenges when you are working for yourself in a one-(wo)man business is that nobody is pushing you. There are no deadlines and nobody other than yourself that you're accountable to. I'm convinced that's where a lot of people get stuck and procrastinate. I totally resonate with how this feels. I come across days where I feel like that, where I'm not motivated, I procrastinate and really don't get anything done.

I know that in order to be successful, I need to show up consistently. This is the time where I go deep within myself and draw that motivation out of myself. I need to dig deep and find it within myself, and the best way to do this is to ask myself WHY am I doing this. My 'why' are my clients. Nothing pushes me more than my clients; helping people break free from their past and from their struggles. I know how debilitating it is; I know how much it sucks when you are just surviving day after day. I will always consistently show up for my clients every day. When I say showing up for my clients, that can be in many different ways – it could be in our one-on-one session, showing up on my YouTube channel, showing up on Facebook or Instagram, showing up by gaining more knowledge so that I can serve my clients even better, or showing up by growing and healing myself. The biggest reward for me is to see the changes in my clients, to see them shine and succeed and thrive in life. Nothing fills my heart more than witnessing these amazing beautiful transformations. This is what drives me. So find your why!

2: PUSH YOURSELF OUT OF YOUR COMFORT ZONE & KEEP GROWING

To reach ultimate success you have to push yourself out of your comfort zone regularly. Of course, it is okay to hang out in your comfort zone for a while and get really good at it. However, there is no growth within your comfort zone. So in order to grow and become more successful, to reach more people and to inspire more people, you have to push yourself out of your comfort zone. I know this is very scary and challenging, but when you have done it, it feels so amazing and so rewarding. I do believe that we need to practice what we preach. My clients that come and see me are pushing out of their own comfort zone by coming to see me and by opening up to me, so I must do the same.

3: DON'T GIVE UP; PUSH THROUGH WHEN IT GETS REALLY HARD

I have experienced many moments where I wanted to throw in the towel and give up. Moments where things haven't worked out. Moments where I have questioned if this will ever work out. Questioning myself if I can ever live my purpose and can make a living out of it. It requires long hours, commitment and definitely patience. It feels so disheartening when you put a lot of effort into something and it doesn't turn out to be successful. I used to feel crushed by it and like a failure. The key thing is to rephrase it, so rather than saying it is a failure, it is a learning. The most successful people have failed more often than you think. The only difference is that they haven't given up. In those moments, it's how you react and deal with it that defines success. Those are the moments that will differentiate you from the others, because most people give up when it gets hard or after they have tried a couple of times.

If you keep pushing through, learn something from it and keep going, you will eventually be successful. I usually always experience these moments just before I have a big breakthrough, but even though I know that, those moments still put me to the test. No matter what, just don't give up.

Conny Wladkowski

Hi, my name is Conny Wladkowski. I'm a hypnotherapist and self-healing coach. I'm also the creator of the SHINE Your Inner Child process, the Break Free From Anxiety EASIER process and the owner of Right Time To Shine Hypnotherapy.

I'm a mother to a beautiful little girl who is my daily inspiration to be the best version of myself. I believe the biggest gift we can give our children is to show them that making mistakes is a part of growth, that our past is not who we are and that we are ALL able to heal! If our children can see the change and healing within us, it will inspire them to know that no matter where they are stuck, they can also heal and create the life they want.

Originally born in Austria, I was on the path of wanting to heal myself and others from a very young age. I was only fifteen when I first studied energy healing, which was my introduction to the world of self-healing and self-empowerment. Having learned multiple modalities and upskilling myself for over thirty years' combined with my own life experiences and healing journey, I have created some magical and profound processes.

I have suffered from trauma and anxiety myself; in fact, for many years I was just surviving. I know how debilitating it can be, but I also know how freeing it is when you can finally live a thriving life. This is why I'm so passionate about doing this work!

Along my journey, I have realised that there are many people suffering from childhood trauma, however most are too scared to open up and heal. Most people are too scared to heal because they don't want to go back and relive the trauma. I totally understand this because this is what was holding me back for many, many years. This led me to create a process where you can heal without having to re-experience it again.

I provide a safe space, free of judgement, full of love and holding. This then allows healing to take place so that you can be the best version of yourself and thrive in life. This is my purpose and I believe and know that this is why I'm here.

Website: www.besthypnotherapymelbourne.com.au
Facebook: www.facebook.com/connywladkowski
Youtube: www.youtube.com/channel/UClSFh4baymeMVpSU-n8Eaow
Instagram: www.instagram.com/right_time_to_shine/
TikTok: vm.tiktok.com/ZSJ9LgtRg/

Emma Romano

FROM FUCKED TO AWESOME

Hey you. Yes, you reading this book. My name is Emma Romano, and firstly, can I just give you a big shout out for choosing this collaboration of women to read from and to spend your precious time with. It's a huge honour for me to be part of such an amazing collaboration – these fellow authors are bloody amazing.

I also LOVE that you have been drawn to the frequency and energy of this book and that you are already aligned (whether you are aware of it or not) to the power of living in a heart-centred, purpose-driven mission. My mission is to prove that it can be a lot easier than you think and that there is so much abundance, passion, love, ease and grace attached to a heart-centred business.

Abundance, you say? Yep. Abundance simply means 'more of', so when you are in alignment with high vibrational thoughts and energy, you simply get MORE of it. More freedom, more love, more health, more money, more clients, more creativity, more joy, more alignment.

Now I feel like I need to give you a warning about my section of this book. I do tend to swear a lot. So if you don't like swear words, just put 'gosh, darn it' in place of the fucks, shits and whatever else I may put on these pages.

The other warning is this; to be within the depths of a heart-centered business, you need to stop any old thoughts caught up in the frequency of scarcity and fear. The *I can't*, *I don't deserve* and especially the, *They will judge me* thoughts. And I can't forget about the 'but it has to be perfect' paradigm. Put them all in the bin. In fact … burn the fuckers. Literally, write down all your shitty beliefs in green pen and burn them.

Okay, so with that said, let's get on with it, shall we? I want to give you as much awesomeness as I can possibly fit into this chapter, so grab a cuppa, have a seat, pick up your highlighter or a pen and paper, and let's do this!

This book is all about heart-centered leadership. To me, this means that when we come from the heart, shit works out. Business flows, health grows, relationships are easier and the dollars flood in. I first started in this business of helping others back in 2015 and have progressed really quickly to an international level where I teach my protocols and mentor healers in business and relationships. I have a huge client base and I teach my own modalities to thousands of people a year, and I do this while still being a mum, wife, daughter, granddaughter, best friend, cousin and business owner.

Now this is the part where I get to impress the shit out of you – well actually, I want to inspire you, not impress you. This little red duck (yes, I'm a ginger) wasn't the brightest of all ducks growing up. In fact, I failed year eight twice and I didn't do the 'normal' year eleven and twelve. But what I lacked in academic smarts, I certainly gained in courage, tenacity and most of all, resilience; all of which would go on to play a key role in my story, which begins back in 2014.

Before I was a business owner, international speaker, facilitator, creator of life-changing processes and a self-healing coach, I used to be a tennis coach and a receptionist (this makes me laugh because I am literally the worst at admin). I was cleaning people's houses and working in pubs pouring beers to the locals. Then one day, I got sick. Really sick, and I was diagnosed with a plethora of issues.

You see, back then I lived a life of people pleasing and co-dependency in my relationships. I needed people to need me. I worked long hours and kept myself incredibly busy. What I was doing really was avoiding the void; the void of time to think. I was actually terrified to feel, so I drank a lot of wine every night. I was heavily involved in anything I could sink my teeth into – the kids' primary school, the softball team, I even enrolled in roller derby, played amateur netball comp and tennis comp. I also made sure I was heavily involved in other people's problems, but not in a good way. Anything to distract myself from my own trauma and negative thoughts and feelings.

Then something big happened that literally made me stop and take a good long hard look at myself and what I was doing to myself, my family and anyone in my life. Get comfy, I'm about to take you on a little tour of my tragedy.

Every Easter, myself and the family would head off camping with other families, and on this particular camping trip, everything was about to change for me and those around me. On our drive this particular night to chilly Ballarat on a windy Thursday evening, I just didn't feel so good. I felt like I was about to get the flu or gastro. Every time I looked up or down, I would get a shooting pain in my head. Then by Saturday evening, my eyesight had gone blurry in my left eye and all of a sudden, I lost the ability to see any colour at all. Fast-track to Tuesday and I was in hospital due to going completely blind in my left eye. I was terrified and was diagnosed with optic neuritis.

By Thursday, I was getting the results of my MRI. I was told that there are four causes of optic neuritis: HIV, AIDS, a brain tumour or multiple sclerosis. *Umm, WHAT THE FUCK*, I thought. I went into a panicked meltdown. I mean, I was the person who looked after everyone else. This couldn't be happening to ME. I certainly NEVER asked others for help.

In the following weeks, I was diagnosed with a list of chronic illnesses: optic neuritis, multiple sclerosis, coeliac disease, depression, anxiety and chronic fatigue. Oh yeah, it was a doozy. I didn't know what I know now, and so I went on the normal route of popping pills and seeing a psychologist and a counsellor. I was just in this perpetual wheel of pain, fear and most of all, hopelessness. I was very close to suicide and some days I couldn't get out of bed or even talk to anyone. I couldn't drive anymore, work or even walk properly.

The year of 2014 – the year of deep shit – was the turning point of my life. Am I grateful for that year? FUCK NO. It was a shit show. I am grateful, however, that I picked myself up, went against the 'norm' and helped myself. I mean, I really did some deep work on myself and literally changed my entire life. I am grateful that I had the heart to find the courage to do things differently and that I now get to inspire people all over the world who are stuck in their own shit.

So what was it? What got me to get off the hamster wheel and stop being a victim to my illnesses? I dropped my eighteen-month-old niece. Yep, my husband handed me my niece and I was leaning against a doorway over a concrete step and I literally went numb in my arms and she dropped. Thank God my husband caught her and she didn't come to any harm.

This was three months after my diagnosis, and from first going blind in my left eye to now three months down the track, I was going downhill fast. I was numb down my right side, in my left foot, both arms and palms of my hands, parts of my face, and the fatigue and depression was all too consuming.

Then the icing on the cake happened … two days after nearly harming my beautiful niece Georgia, my son Ben and I were sitting on the couch one midafternoon watching *How to Train Your Dragon*. I was still in my PJs (I very rarely got out of them or even showered) and Ben looked at me square in the eyes and said, "Mummy, I love it when you are sick." I was like, *What the fuck?* He said, "Because you are still." This hit me hard right in the centre of my chest. You see, I've been through some tragedy in my life. I ran from my first husband with my one-year-old, Jack, and a belly full of Ben, my second baby. Ben was born at twenty-six weeks gestation, only three weeks after I fled London and the father of my boys to come back home to Australia. All I ever wanted was to be a mother, and it took having MS to realise that I wasn't even present throughout it. So this was the turning point. It wasn't the illness, it was the kids.

I went back to my neurologist begging to know when I was going to improve or heal. I mean, I was religiously taking my medication day and night, so I wanted to know – when would I start feeling better? I was told in no uncertain terms that I wouldn't heal from any of these issues and that I would most likely be in a wheelchair within six months. Hang on, WHAT?

"FUCK THAT."

These were the last two words that I ever spoke to that neurologist. That was July 2014 and I haven't been back. I'm not in a wheelchair, I have absolutely no symptoms and I am thriving in life.

I chose not to believe or be convinced that I couldn't heal. I knew in my heart of hearts that the body has an innate ability to heal itself and that there are certain things that can block that: environment, negative and stuck emotions, shit food and limiting belief systems, karmic contracts and past life woo-woo stuff (just to name a few). I call all of these self-poisoning. And I have to tell you – healing the illnesses or diseases in my body were the easy part. Healing the self-loathing, anger, fear and the shame of who I was? That part took years.

I am eternally grateful for my courage and tenacity and my self-healing abilities, but most of all, for thinking and acting outside of the 'box'. And guess what? You have this capability too. Everyone does, we are born with it. And it's as simple as tapping back into the high vibration of healing instead of the low vibration of illness.

This is what I do now. I pull people out of the shitty box and guide them quickly, lovingly and sometimes with an almighty shove into the awesome and heart-centred box. You see, when you come from heart and love, you heal and thrive. When you come from fear, limited self-belief and low self-love for yourself … you get sick.

So that's enough about the past in this short chapter; I want to bring you into the now. After I healed myself, I knew that I had to share this with the world. It would be selfish if I didn't and so this is what I now teach others all over the world.

You see, what I do is very different to others. I have discovered, experimented and researched, and I have been changing the frequency and vibration of this universe by using five key ingredients to create instant, deep and long-lasting change. In any work I do, either teaching my modalities or business mentoring, I use all the dimensions of the human and spirit form. I work with the conscious mind, unconscious mind and energy, at a cellular level and at a soul level. Every process I facilitate or teach includes all five of these dimensions, which is why what I do works so deeply, instantly and with profound long-lasting results.

When I first started out with my business in 2016, I quit my job in June of that year and took the plunge. I was excited, exhilarated yet terrified because I had this scarcity mindset. It's a fear energy, not a heart-centred energy, so I struggled. I struggled with money, clients and energy, I was riddled with fear of judgment and the list goes on and on.

In the first two years, I made less than $20,000 which isn't enough to sustain a life here in Australia. I then heard that little voice in my head (yes, my son Jack's fifteen-year-old voice) telling me that I was doing this all wrong and that I had to do my business from the heart instead of from fear. Heart is a high vibration; fear is literally an illusion and runs on zapping energy, not giving energy.

I made some major mistakes in the early days of starting up this business. The mistakes were that I came from scarcity and competition. When

I was in that vibration, I really struggled to find clients, get referrals or even ask for money. My heart was in the right place of wanting to help, but I just didn't put that heart-centered vibe into the rest of my business.

When you are working with people's soul, wounds, heart, and unconscious mind, the only way to do this work is from the heart. When you let money and scarcity and competition come into play, it simply doesn't work or you'll find that you easily jump into the hustle or desperation. When you realise that everything is energy and that everything has its own frequency, you build relationships from love. You build a relationship with your business, money, dreams, goals and your past from love. You step out of being the 'victim' and start using your past to empower your present and future self.

Where healers can fall into a trap is by 'doing' their amazing business with old belief systems and programs that they are unaware of. You see, what I find interesting is that we are only really 5% aware of what we are doing, and the rest of the 95% is all old programming which actually comes from negative emotions and limiting beliefs that we have been through, witnessed or been hypnotised to believe in during our early years or from past lives.

When I studied the laws of the universe, I learnt that it is all about HEART. The universe is actually IN our OWN heart; it is our heart centre. So, you amazing and gorgeous soul, yes – you ARE the universe. And I have something huge to tell you … You are constantly acting out your belief systems and proving yourself right when you manifest your life. It's bloody scary and thrilling at the same time. So if you look at your life and notice what is swimming along beautifully right now, it's because you have a belief system around it and you have created it from a heart-centred space. You rockstar!

BUT, all the shit going on in your life right now, like – *I'm broke, I hate my work, struggle in relationships* – you have also created a belief system around and you have created out of fear. Remember, fear is the opposite of being heart-centred.

The amazing news is that you can switch it up, I promise. I know so, because this is what I personally did and have helped over a thousand clients and taught thousands of practitioners and therapists through. It's a lot easier than you think and I am going to share it with you in the rest of this chapter.

First we must remember that this universe is based on abundance, love, creation and joy. That is our HEART CENTRE and if you think of everything in the terms of frequencies, vibrations and energy, everything becomes much easier. Even if you do something as simple as cooking a meal for yourself, all of the ingredients will have a vibration, a frequency and energy to them. Fresh organic produce will hold a higher frequency, as a healthier option. Yet if you are cooking with white sugar and processed foods, these will hold a very low frequency, and a low vibration. In other words, one is very healthy and life-giving, and the other is dead and won't give us life, literally taking life away from us. The same applies to your business.

If you are excited (high frequency) but scared of judgement (low frequency), these are the ingredients that are going into your business. Everything you think flows into an emotion, and that emotion vibrates out of you as a frequency. So, what are you vibrating? Here is the most basic, yet most important process you can be aware of and do for yourself in every part of your life:

Write down on a piece of paper in green pen (green is for releasing) all of the fears and limiting beliefs you have, and all of the things that are blocking you from living in your full freedom and abundant life with ease and grace. If you were to rate each thought, belief or feeling out of ten ('10' being a high vibe and '0' being the lowest and most debilitating vibe), what would you rate them?

For example:

Fraud – 1

Judgement – 2

Fear – 0

'I don't know how' – 2

'I can't do it' – 1

Jealousy – 3

These are your ingredients to your heart-centred business. This is the reason that healers and therapists struggle; it's STUCK energy. You could call it 'playing victim' to these negative thought forms. So, what if you were to switch it up to a higher, yet realistic, vibration, and numbered them also? Here's an example:

'I'm learning how to do this business' – 7

'I'm okay with who I am' – 9

'I'm practising being me' – 10

'I am important to the matrix of people's healing journey' – 10

Now look at your ingredients. Do you think with this kind of vibe and mindset that life would be easier or harder? EASIER. I know, because this is how I switched not just my health, but my relationships and my thriving business. It is a lot easier than you have been led to believe, and guess what? This planet needs more heart-centered therapists and healers. Welcome to our container ship, darling heart. Thank you for your time. Much love to you, Emma.

Emma Romano

As an international self-healing coach, business mentor and trainer, my soul's mission is to raise the vibration and frequency of humanity through supporting healers to become thriving practitioners!

I do this through my extensive experience with clients and practitioners, as well as the deep modalities I've created that use the 'five dimension-method' which work very uniquely to any other modalities and methods out there.

I've spoken across Australia and internationally, spreading my message of peace, self-healing and kindness, and bringing awareness to these new modalities available within my multiple programs: The Family Freedom Protocol, Delete Reset and Timeline Reset.

My expertise is in treating clients with negative emotions such as depression, anxiety, PTSD and limiting beliefs, using my own creation Timeline Reset, hypnotherapy, energy work, and life coaching. With these modalities I'm able to get to the very core issue of my client's problem and facilitate their self-healing process.

In 2014 I was diagnosed with the debilitating disease of MS, which led to chronic fatigue and saw me looping in fear and depression. After hearing from multiple medical professionals that I should prepare myself for a wheelchair, I decided to seek my own answers and take matters into my own hands.

After extensive years of study and research, I devised a program for clients and therapists to share these powerful tools of self-healing with them. I hope to spread my powerful message globally; that working with the conscious and unconscious mind at a soul level using hypnotherapy, mindset, energy work and lifestyle is crucial if people are serious about overcoming their illness and blockages and truly desire to live a life of health and happiness.

Changing our mindset at the unconscious level is a very powerful healing modality as it allows for the release and transformation of negative thought patterns and negative emotions that are trapped and toxic to the body. Through this work, I strive to empower therapists with the tools they need to help their clients really thrive in life in the fastest and most graceful way possible.

Website: www.emmaromano.com.au
Email: emma@emmaromano.com.au
Facebook: www.facebook.com/healwithemmaromano
Instagram: www.instagram.com/healwithemmaromano

Luzette Singh-Williams
THE ROAD TO EMPOWERING YOUTH

At thirty-five years old my heart began to beat with a slow, dull sound and vibration, and I knew I had to take steps to revitalise myself. If I was to hold space for so many, I needed to know how to hold my own first and to relearn who I was. I had creativity and potential that had not yet been explored. It was then that I realised that the only way to access this 'power' was to move the walls and boulders I had placed in front of me through self-imposed barriers built up through fear, conditioning and resistance. I always say the only person who knows what you really need is yourself; you just have to listen.

To listen isn't to sit still for five minutes and to wait for a voice to speak up. To listen is to sit and sit some more, until the silence begins to swirl with the thoughts and emotions that have not had a chance to rise, come up and present themselves to you. The power lies in looking them in the eye and deciding if this is to make you or break you. Does the storm enter into your veins and allow you to have a dose of that life vitamin to spark up the internal engine? Or does it occur, pass, then leave you feeling wounded, vulnerable and powerless … a missed opportunity?

As my curiosity for yoga began years prior, I began to learn more about myself and my place in the world through the stillness that it brought me. When the seed was planted in my mind that I may teach, I thought, *I don't know anything about yoga, but I know how I feel when I do it.* I know how it feels to play and what it does to your body and mind, so what if I was to spread this around and share it with others? It was then in 2018 that fate led me on a path to undergo the most amazing training with Rainbow Yoga in Australia. Those words – "I don't know anything about … but I know how I feel when I do …" is the classic statement that can make or break any presented opportunity.

Youth Yoga was created in the dark where my eyes had to be closed so I could feel what I needed to step into. I had often reflected on my youthful experiences and like many of us, I had plenty, and I also had a wonderful ability to use these experiences to share with others. It dawned on me in 2018 that I had a gift, an ability to create meaningful experiences through my own often challenging experiences. I reflected on the absence of tools to help me navigate life as a young person, and to receive help we had to ask for it. But if you didn't know you were struggling, how could you request such a service?

New Zealand has an alarming suicide rate, and in March 2018, I was listening to the radio and an ad was highlighting the suicide statistics. On this particular morning, I paid more attention because it pulled on my heart strings more and more, and as I listened to the ad on the radio, I also heard a voice within me saying, *What are you going to do about it?* My internal response was, *Nothing … I am one person … what can I do?* That question sat with me and the voice got louder and louder, until it took over the steering wheel and began to drive me in the direction of change and empowerment. Not only for myself, but for all of the young people I was to meet.

Low self-esteem, body image, endless thoughts, anxiety, fear, identity, stress, emotions, friendships, pressure, uncertainty, family dynamics, sibling dynamics – these are some of the issues our young people face and I knew I could touch on these topics in a lighthearted and supporting manner and so I began to do just this.

Often we are told to 'lead by example', but what happens when that example isn't a good one? So, leading by experience and lessons becomes a great asset when helping our young people to grow. I teach by being vulnerable in my classes, by digging deep and using those once crippling personal experiences that become stepping blocks and metaphorical tools. One of my favourite classes to teach is about trust and asking questions such as, "Do you trust yourself and your gut feeling?" – that feeling you can't explain but is a signal that comes from the body, guiding you as an internal compass. As I reflect on my youth, there were a number of times I did not listen to my gut feeling, leading me to many unpleasant experiences and saying yes when I wanted to say no. My goal was to set out and provide tools to be used before the experiences happened, and to make those connections using their own 'body intelligence' so they had more of a guide when making decisions.

The pivotal moment that germinated the seed was realising that I was a hypocritical parent, hanging up quotes on the fridge with hope and wonder, yet my actions reflected fear, conditional happiness and resistance to my true calling. As I spun out these words to my children trying to inspire them, that little voice from deep down said, *But you are not happy and you are not in alignment with your purpose, because your soul is tired.* And as any good conversation goes, the response was, *I am too old to start from scratch and the uncertainty of running my own business is too scary. But maybe when the kids get older I might, or in a few years.* It's that same convincing argument that tends to push our dreams and desires out by another day, another week, another year and another decade.

I remember rushing from work to catch the train, then heading out to pick up my son. As I was chatting to the teacher selling my fake story about how happy I was achieving so much, a young boy walked up to me casually and said, "Your car is rolling down the hill." I turned and ran to the car but the door was locked! In slow motion I watched it getting closer to the other car, until I could unlock it and yank up the handbrake, managing to stop it from crashing with centimetres to spare.

To this day, that moment has haunted me. I felt like it was a crazy metaphor for my life, my body becoming weak and slowly rolling down to an inevitable incident. As I reflect on that moment three years on, I often think about how much I was trying to do at the time and how the one thing I didn't do was put the handbrake of life up. I had also developed a weak immune system and I had the worst cough I have ever experienced for a period of three months, paired with extreme fatigue. I felt my body was so toxic from repressed emotions, overworking and trying to please everyone, and the only way it knew how to come out and for me to pay attention was through inflammation and messages in the most uncomfortable way possible.

What did I need to stop? I had to stop denying the internal dialogue and pretending that I could do it all. I needed things to cease in order to become grounded, and that is when I said goodbye to the character I was playing and decided to take a risk and pursue a dream to empower young people. I literally had hit rock bottom in the sense that my energy and my soul was so tired, I had nothing to lose. I had to push those fears aside and stop creating a scary future that had not yet unfolded. I was a survivor and now I wanted to become a creator.

Human beings are extremely good at jumping ahead into the future and creating false realities that cripple us. Our body reacts to our thoughts, and we often create a mental prison for ourselves, so the questions that began to surface for me were, *Can I jump with purpose and more direction to steer the ship?* If we as a species are so good at creating a crumbling reality that hasn't even been created yet but keeps us in our place, then can we too create one with safety nets that catch us and then transport us to another platform, long after that one has crumbled? I think so.

Some platforms are not meant to last forever, and some opportunities are only meant to serve a purpose before leaving us. The gift of human imagination is so magical; we need to go back to that time when anything was possible and everything was achievable. Back to that knowing from birth to this current moment, where we have never truly stayed the same and yet we have survived. Our teeth fell out when we were younger, but they were not long replaced. Our body actually expanded in height, and in a vast amount of growth internally and externally, we survived. It meant that we no longer had to tippy-toe to get the cookie jar from the top shelf, and perhaps we even resisted these changes, but nevertheless they occurred and we adapted accordingly. More importantly, they offered new opportunities for us to explore.

The main roadblock that we face is that we tend to look for these huge moments that will give us the 'green light' to move forward. Sometimes we need to trust a little bit more that we will always have our own backs, through willpower and an innate ability to want to survive and thrive.

There is such beauty working with children; I can't even begin to describe the joy and contentment I feel when I have conversations with young people. This is where I'm in my element, and I may not know it all or have experienced it all, but I do my best to share and to hold space for those who are working with me. The fate of humanity rests upon our beautiful children and young adults being held in a space that can back-pedal and regenerate more hope and love. To change the frequency of their stunted growth due to their experiences, into beautiful works of art that open and engage.

Below is Youth Yoga's teaching timeline, highlighting the need and success of my heart-centred business:

2018 – 80 students in a year

2019 – 320 students in a year

2020 – 600 students in a year

2021 – 1100 students in a year, 180 teachers and 120 corporate employees

We each have our own frequency but I certainly had to find mine, and I encourage you to find yours. Can you get out of your head and into your body? Does it cringe at the thought of moving in a certain direction? Are you able to trust the answers it sends you, even if they are feelings and not words? The best comment I was thrown when I first started on this path was, "Why don't you get a real job?" I will never forget those words and how they made me feel; I felt the fear creeping up again and trying to consume me back into a 'safe' place. I had a choice to make – do I crumble and retreat, or do I take those words, mould them into a step and move on up?

I had many friends and family members who supported my decision and I had many in which I sparked their fear of the unknown and so they were filled with doubt for my new adventure. I was then forced to back myself and to trust my own internal compass. I had schools/teachers and parents who did not think that their child would be interested in anything to do with yoga or mindfulness, and yet I was able to capture their attention and show huge results in their wellbeing. I had students sharing how they were feeling, working together with other students, connecting, letting down their guard, laughing, playing, being kids and learning at the same time.

I had numerous students who were self-proclaimed bullies becoming friends with those that they bullied. Students that were self-harming began to ask for help, and students started to speak up about traumatic events that had an impact on them mentally to this day. This was not asked in the class, there was no expectation at all to discuss this, but it was a by-product of the breakthrough in our classes, and the ability to create a safe, non-judgemental space that let that internal voice be heard and gently guide them towards exploring that further with respective professionals within the school.

To run a heart-centred business is a business that is the life force and blood supply of one's being. An organ that runs the show, filled with joy and love, and decisions made from a central space that benefits everything around her and not just for one cause. A heart-centred space that knows the heartbeat of others beats differently, and when we offer instruments to help the flow of their beat, this is how one becomes empowered. It's not about 'one size fits all', it's about presenting an opportunity and holding space for that person to understand what sound will resonate with them, to be in harmony with their organic self.

"Create a life that you love so much you don't need a break from it," – that wonderful quote that often seems like a dream – is possible. If you want to create a heart-centred business, I would say dip your toes in first, and allow that water to show you a vision of what it might look like to manifest this into reality. Take it slow, do not try to achieve so much so soon, as you will be sure to miss the simple pleasures that come with beginning to be more aligned with yourself and your purpose.

Celebrate the failures, the mistakes and the lessons, and laugh and dance to the bumps along the way, for they teach us how to step left and right as we go along the path. Take the fear and remember it emits the same feeling as excitement – one can cripple you and the other can have you giggling like a child.

Start small, create a vision board, and get to the point where you can taste it. Enter that space where the thought of pursuing your purpose gives you a tingle. Definitely make sure the bills are paid, have a job on the side and build it up slowly to take the pressure off yourself and your dependents. Often we can be left feeling guilty for stepping off the conveyor belt to explore our options, so if you are practical then it will be more enjoyable. When I first started, I worked a full-time job to begin with and started small, then moved to a part time job and slowly started to visualise my goals.

Take breaks; remember this comes from your heart, a space of wonder and beauty. It means that there needs to be a balance of energy – give and take, work and play. To listen to the beat of the drum should never be at the sacrifice of your own beat. A heart centred business rocking out to techno music (multitasking) will eventually tire you out.

Be vulnerable and share your experiences, allowing yourself to be seen and heard through your work. Allow others to hear your story, and grow from every experience that life has presented to you. Take the lessons of what it was meant to teach you, each often painful but necessary for your growth. That layer that you peel off can often be the support blanket that others need to be held in, to understand how to make peace with their past and experiences.

I always tell my students, "I am not here to save you or magically make your problems disappear; but I am planting seeds within your mind to remind you that you will always have OPTIONS. I am not a teacher, but a student of life that is always learning, always evolving, not resisting but embracing each part of my being that unfolds over time. I don't know what it is like to be you, but I have experiences that have taught me something. Often we can't change our circumstances, but we can hold control over our reactions to things and that is where we begin to regain our power."

I have created a heart-centred business by acknowledging that the source is ultimately what is important, whatever that might look like for you. It is often about taking away those distractions such as, *I am successful when I make x-amount of money. I am successful when everyone in the classroom smiles and laughs*, or, *I am successful when I am recognised on the street*. These statements provided are all centred around me and how the business is relevant to stroking my ego. You are heart-centred when you have held space to let people become who they are and more importantly allow them to pause and reset. Heart-centred is when you no longer have to chase something, it will find you.

Becoming an entrepreneur is a horrifying, fantastic experience. It means that there are many times when you literally do not know what is around the corner; how exciting to invite the element of surprise back into your life. It's sometimes staring at your bank account thinking, *How can I perform magic to change these numbers?* Money is a number, a set of digits displayed on your screen that often dictates your entire life, your moods, fear and excitement, and yet you need to get away from this often, and allow your passion and drive to be the motivation.

I remember starting out in a kindergarten and teaching ten wonderful children. I was then asked, How much do you charge per class?" Umm, no-one had ever told me how to figure out what I was worth, and so the journey began … charging a little but giving a lot. Eventually, as one begins to listen to the beat of the drum, your heart knows your worth, and your time, passion, energy and late nights need to be rewarded accordingly, and more importantly, unapologetically.

Whether we know it or not, our children are our biggest teachers. Their purity as it enters into this world allows us to relive joy and unconditional love, and evoking change through love and guidance to help this young person go forth in the world is such a rewarding experience for both the student and the teacher. When we empower our young people, it takes away the need to steal others' power through negative means such as physical violence, verbal and emotional abuse to those more vulnerable than us. When we are in our own power and self-esteem is flowing, we are then nurturing what it is we need.

"It's not about how much you do, but how much love you put into what you do that counts."
— **Mother Teresa**

Luzette Singh-Williams

Luzette; 'a small light' … That was the name I was gifted upon entering this earth. A Greek name bestowed onto an Indian baby, would shine brighter than I ever thought in 2018. I am Luzette Singh-Williams, the sole director and sole teacher of Youth Yoga Ltd a heart-centred business I ventured upon with a vision to empower children and young adults in every sense of the word.

I run programmes in schools using yoga and mindfulness, specifically catered to youth. My classes involve a combination of play, movement, kinesthetic learning and stillness to teach my carefully thought out lesson plans. Each class is created with the intention of planting mindful seeds and opening their awareness through curiosity and connection to oneself and each other. In turn, this promotes a non-competitive, supportive, fun learning environment to touch on topics for personal evolutionary growth.

I am a graduate in psychology and sociology, a children's/young person's yoga and mindfulness teacher, taught by the amazing team at Rainbow Yoga from Australia, who I dedicate immense gratitude to for the stepping stone in my journey. Through their training, I unleashed parts of myself that completely changed my perspective in life, and my creativity and drive to empower young adults increased tenfold.

In my adult body, my inner child dictates my life in a positive way. I have gone against the grain in every aspect of my life and have been rewarded greatly for doing so. When I teach, I bring high energy, great vibes and a huge ability to build rapport, having worked with and met so many wonderful people in my life, both challenging and nurturing. I run workshops for teachers and corporate teams highlighting the importance of self-care with an emphasis on how our 'internal lack' can be projected outward.

I am the creator of Youth Yoga affirmation cards, designed to represent more diversity within many communities. I have taken yoga poses and positive affirmations and paired them together to create a beautiful link between the physical and mental realm. This then helps one to shift their mental state when they can move their physical body and repeat a positive affirmation.

I am a self-healing coach and reiki practitioner with a natural ability to feel energy, be drawn to those that need assistance and bring the light up out of the darkness. I work with my clients to show them that they have the answers, but together we create a wonderful space to allow these answers or revelations to be experienced.

I share my journey with my beautiful children, Ruka and Shaan, and my amazing husband Atama, who helped me navigate this ride, to which I can now proudly add co-author of this amazing book to my accomplishments.

This is my journey of the dance that created the opening act of my new career/lifestyle. Take from it what you will, but remember if you are reading this then something inside of you is already wanting to hear, "It is time."

Facebook: www.facebook.com/Youth-Yoga-Ltd-2079678078727147/
Website: www.youthyoga.co.nz
Instagram: https://www.instagram.com/youthyoga_ltd/

Leanne Carson

FORKS IN THE ROAD

H ello, I am Lee. Who am I?

Well, a beauty therapist by trade, if you were to ask me what I do.

I'm a mother of three. Independent, strong, charismatic, and a loyal friend that loves deeply. I'm a spiritual healer and an aura reader, amongst many of my other talents or gifts, if you will. How did I get to be where I am? Well, to be honest, I don't think one chapter would quite cut it, so how about I start with where I actually am now …

I am a year and half out of a twenty-year relationship. I am an attempted suicide, domestic (and violent) abuse survivor, from two separate relationships. My days at the moment are still a battle on the daily, a battle to heal and move forward from the most horrendous treatment I have ever endured and continue to endure. Almost six months ago, on my fortieth birthday, my ex and the father of my two youngest children turned up on my doorstep, collected my children and never returned them. He removed them from my care and poisoned them against me, destroying them and part of myself in the process.

In and amongst all of this, today I woke to the sounds of birds chirping – a new sound I have not heard throughout the winter months, and music to my ears – spring is about to spring upon us, and I am so ready to embrace this and hug a tree! A new awakening awaits me; a new birthing, a new cleansing, and newer and greater things to look forward to. This may sound a little weird and quirky but this is everything that is soul nurturing for myself as I get up and face the day; a day where I face yet another battle within myself as I go to work at the same school my children attend yet I am not allowed to see them. Yep, yes indeed, you did read that correctly. And as you read this you may be asking, *How can this be?* And as I am writing this, I too am asking the very same question. So perhaps I will explain, and maybe as I write it all down, we might all come to understand together, maybe?

Many times over I have restructured the words for my chapter, as every day a new series of events occur and throw my whole world into yet another tail and head spin. I've wondered, *Do I focus more on sharing my work life or personal life?* It just so happens that as of recently, I am now able to do both. Since starting to write these words, I have since made the choice to resign from my job at the school; not an easy to decision to make, as it's a job that I love and that I am fantastic at, but to walk into a school every day and not be able to speak with my own children was a nightmare, and I've decided that this is how I take my power back! This is freeing, liberating and exciting for me, as I move into my new job opportunity, and a job that I love just as much.

I completed my Certificate II in Business eight years ago, when my youngest child was two years old. I was desperate to find some form of purpose in my life other than as a housewife and mother. Don't get me wrong, I did enjoy being a stay-at-home mum for the most part, but my husband worked away a lot, and I would only be left with a small allowance weekly to get through the week with no access to bank accounts. Being on my own with three children daily was hard work, as any stay-at-home mother or father can relate to, and at the time I just thought this was normal – husband works away, wifey plays house and is just given money for the groceries, fuel, medications, phone bill, etc. The weekly things. Yet I had a burning hunger for something more for myself; I wanted a career, something for myself. Something I could fall back on if my marriage failed.

So with the child support I received D from my first child's father (it took thirteen years to receive anything, but that is another chapter), I enrolled two-year-old Miss L into day care and myself into TAFE. I was proud of myself for completing my certificate but I chose it by process of elimination, and it was not something I could find myself in career wise. I quickly learned that me and technology were not the best of mates, but because I didn't want to stop learning something for myself, I ended up applying for the new Certificate II in Community Pharmacy the follow-ing week. Again, I was proud of myself for achieving this, but this was not something I could see myself doing, as I had always leaned more so towards the holistic side and natural therapies. This was where everything came to a halt for me again, and I resumed my role as a full-time stay-at-home mum, as my son was also becoming quite ill and hospital visits were becoming extremely frequent. Master C has the nickname bubble boy, which sums it up in a nutshell.

I then started to fall back into a depressive state. But you are mum and housewifey, you just pull your shit together and do what is expected of you. I was suffering badly. I loved my children, but I needed more!

It took a lot of courage to ask my husband to front the $5,000 that was required to put me through beauty school. Not only because of the money side of things but because of the change up in what was needed from him to be there for the children after school two days a week for the year that it would take to complete the course. Most of those days are a blur as it was hectic busy for myself, with the studying after-hours and the time taken to fit in the required hours of model practises, but I completed the course and found what I truly loved to do and am fantastic at. The dining room in our tiny Jenga house became my work station, I created my business name Beauty-full-lee, and started taking on clients. *Wow,* I thought, *I am finally making my own money and fitting clients in around the children.* I was happy, I was uplifted, I had grand plans to further my career – yes, a career, not a job – and I had a self-made business that was all mine.

We were rapidly outgrowing our tiny home; Miss L and Master C were still sharing a room, now at the age of seven and ten, so it was time to move on. Up into the Hills to further chase my dreams, still burning for more, in a house with a room that I could work from flourish in my amazingness. This came with many a challenge and struggle; my eldest telling me two weeks before we moved that she was not coming with us. I was devastated. I thought, *Have I made the right choice?* A beautiful life in the Hills, but at the resentment of Miss M? Again, my struggles began, with that dark depression creeping upon me again, and like a black hole in the galaxy, our entire family unit was sucked up, sucked in and started to spiral. For the longest of time I believed that I was solely responsible for this; husband no longer had any time for me, he too suffered a breakdown and had to take time from work, and the arguments were horrendous. I felt so much guilt every time he would take a dig at me, chipping away at me more and more every day. I'd ask him, "What does your weekend look like?" a pretty common question for a wife to ask a husband.

He'd reply with "I'm fixing this place up, cleaning the ever-growing yard," with little snaps at me in frustration and a force behind it that said it was my fault that he was so overworked now. Then his OCD kicked in big time, and I couldn't do anything right; nothing at all was good enough or it was not done properly, I was in the way or my things were in the way. I started dreading him coming home, thinking I hadn't done enough.

For two years we had been living in the Hills, and I had been hiding myself away in the house for most of it. I went back to having to ask permission to put fuel in my car (sorry, his car), etc. By this stage, I no longer even liked myself, and I was spending more and more time hidden in the back room, away from him, which meant I was also hiding from my children too. I could hear them laughing all the time, whilst I was being invisible, and this is where he took his action. "Mum is not well, Mum is in a mood," blah blah blah. The kids taught to think that something was wrong with me, which led me to ask, *Is there something wrong with me?* I then heard about this HER centre, a women's centre offering beautiful therapies, yoga, meditation, sound therapies and reiki healings. I was asked by a friend if I would like to learn reiki with them. I absolutely did. Upon doing my level one, my confidence was returning, and I joined the meditation and yoga weekly. I was learning so much about myself, and I was able to share safely that I was wanting to leave my marriage but didn't yet know how to. I completed my reiki two attunement and my world exploded. My self-worth exploded, and my husband hated this even more.

At this time, I secured employment at the local pub. I was back in kitchens, something I had done from the age of fifteen, and the hours were long. The whole experience was challenging as I was battling this horrendous home life that had become so toxic and I was not able to keep holding it together, but I was making money and I had a plan. This was my moment, and I started putting my plan into action. I soon found myself living in the back room permanently, and I couldn't breathe! But because I was working nights, it meant we mostly didn't see each other, however this also meant I didn't see my children either, and God knows what he was saying to them. It was Miss L's birthday and I had gone all-out as I usually did, with all the beautiful presents – she my little artist, gets it from her Mumma – and her birthday party was all organised as always. I texted my husband G from the back room, *Have you gotten anything for her to open tomorrow?*

No, I was just going to take her shopping, he replied. Knowing he wouldn't have, I was glad she would have something to open in the morning, but then they ended up going to birthday lunch without me. I felt discarded, invisible. My kids led to believe that something's wrong with Mum again … I am soon packing my bags several times a week and escaping to friends' houses to get away from him, but the kids stay with him, leaving him more time to do his work on them. "Look, Mum's leaving us, Mum's not okay." No, I certainly am not okay, and what he is doing is not okay, but no-one can help me. I have strict instructions not to talk to his family anymore; they were all checking in on him and he began to feel like a victim. So I was told to stop talking to his family, but now my safety net has been torn away. Who can help me? I then lost my job, as the pub shut down and I was left completely broke as he restricted and tightened the rules on spending. By this stage, I am no longer ashamed and afraid to be vulnerable and ask for help. I can't do this without some form of help. I asked him to leave the property, as he has family and other people to stay with. I needed to stay to get the kids to school, and it was officially over – I had nothing left in me. He then threatened his life and self-harmed, leaving me to feel guilty again, thinking I have created this, but I decided I am not staying for this. It was not getting better and I knew it never would at this point. The children, however, have now been led to believe that I hurt their father and that I was capable of this – "Look, something's wrong with Mum, and now she is hurting our dad!" I can't tell them he did this to himself, because that is not something they should have to hear, so I continue to allow them to believe I did it … They now know that I didn't, but the damage was done.

Six weeks later he moved back in, which again did not end well. I was cornered in a room, distressed, and screaming "Leave me the fuck alone!! Get away from me." He was blocking the door – *Why will he not listen to me ever?* – and.I am pleading for him to let me out of the room. It was awful.

From there, I left. I was offered a rental in Roleystone, around the corner from the school, and did shared care of the kids, week on, week off – fifty-fifty. It was a good manageable arrangement that I thought would allow the healing to begin for all, so we could all move forward with our lives in the most positive of ways, but I soon realised I was wrong. I left with not a cent to my name and no car, but I am adamant that I can do this, and that I can rebuild my life. Rebuilding I definitely am, but the rest of it is still so uncertain.

I am not free from him; he has punished me by taking my children from me. But amongst all of this, I have resigned from my job, I am taking my power back, I have a new job opportunity that I am excited about that can open many doors for the future, and it's also freed up some time for me to fall back into the spiritual and self-growth side of things I love to do. I have found my tribe, I have found my sisterhood, and I found myself!

I am now about to move house again, as i have to share accommodation and will no longer have a space to work out of, but my plan is to turn my business into a local mobile service. There is no such thing as *I cannot do.* in my world; through all of these life experiences, one thing I have learned is that nothing is ever concrete and solid, and life is ever changing. I believe that being a heart-centred leader means inspiring others to keep on going no matter what curve balls life may throw at you. I have stepped up and into my life, giving my all through the hardest of challenges, and there have been days when I wanted to give up. But now there is nothing that holds me back. I've chosen to share my story on social media and have received multiple personal messages from others that have experienced similar struggles and don't not know where to turn, and if I can reach just one other person and possibly help them through, then my story has shown its purpose.

I have also thrown myself back into my home business which means everything to me. Beauty therapy and reki energy works; this is my passion, helping others to find their inner healing. I have so much to offer, but I know that this is not where it all ends for me. I am passionate about furthering my future within helping others to rebuild and find healing within similar circumstances, and whilst I am not too sure yet how it will look as I am still doing the work myself, I know that my painful past is my way to paving a happier and more giving future.

Whilst I know many people are inspired by my strength and motivation, I don't yet feel like I've yet made it as a leader. But I do know that I am completely inspired every day by those are around me whom are leading the way, through their businesses, careers and their everyday lives, just by being magnificent and sharing their power and knowledge with others. Every day I am truly blessed to know some of the most incredible ladies ever to walk this earth, and I aspire to one day be making a true impact in the lives of other women too.

May the journey continue … I am excited to embrace what lays ahead for me, and I continue to hold the hope that my precious children will find their way back to the love of their mother once they understand that they too have been the victim of domestic abuse.

Leanne Carson

I'm Lee. A mother of three with all of the wifey/mother experience that's essential to supporting a fairytale life. AKA, being a good mumma, wife, daughter-in-law, aunty; all of the things that we're told are required for us to be and that are expected of us.

Well, all of this put me in a box, a box I know is familiar to many. Despite being happy in my mothering role – I'm a nurturing soul, so this was never the struggle – I desired to change this conforming narrative and the struggle it puts on remembering your own self and who you really are underneath it all.

But as I tried to find myself again, the world shook for my family – my husband, my children, my in-laws and all of our friends around us. I went looking for myself and it was not liked. And so this is my story.

Facebook: www.facebook.com/beauty-full-lee
Instagram: www.instagram.com/beautyfulee

Karen Swainson

HURT PEOPLE, HURT PEOPLE
FORGING A NEW PATH FORWARD

n times past there was a sweet, innocent, vibrant young soul who had a dance in her every step. Her cheery voice would greet others warmly, making them feel welcomed and at home. Always willing to help in any way she could, her smile touched the eyes and the hearts of many. There was a sense of wonder and curiosity about her and how she viewed the world around her.

She brought this with her throughout life, though after a traumatic experience not of her own accord, a shadow started seeping into different aspects of her life. She felt her heart close up, her voice restricted and her light dulled as she became more reserved, her laughter not as joyful nor so frequently expressed. Her thirst for adventure and fun was more reckless, seeking the thrill of feeling alive and on the edge. The many walls she had slowly built around herself to create a greater sense of safety had begun to restrict her sense of freedom within.

It would be many years before she courageously faced her shadows and the intricate web that it had woven through all the areas of her life; returning gradually to her fullness with faith and trust restored, where *she loved and accepted herself, knowing and feeling safe within body once more.*

Her wisdom was that of the heart. Her song was to the beat of nature's rhythm, and so the healing began.

Have you ever heard of the saying 'hurt people, hurt people'? For me, through my own experience, it wasn't until it came full circle that I truly appreciated the depth to its meaning. I understood that when one person had been hurt, whether mentally, physically and/or emotionally, it left an imprint and that they would carry the pain of those events with them. What I didn't realise was how much my unresolved pain or trauma was playing such a major part throughout my entire life, obscuring my thoughts, my emotional responses and informing my behaviours. The effect of these unresolved emotional events surfaced in unhealthy and unsupportive ways. Filtering into all areas of my life, especially in my role as a mother.

Having children can be the most rewarding and honoured role. We are gifted these tiny souls that rely on us to hold, guide, nurture and love them as they find their own feet in the world. They are born with the purest of intentions, absorbing and mirroring the environment in which they are placed. They are also our greatest teachers.

I was blissfully unaware of the range of emotions I could feel, nor did I understand their full function. Becoming a parent, I was relearning these at the same time my beauties were experiencing theirs. They ignited something within me, knowing myself in ways I may not have thought possible or even knew existed. I'd often wonder if I was getting it right. Feeling stretched and out of my depth, trying to navigate situations that I knew shaped and imprinted the very essence of who they are. I experienced many of their firsts alongside them, filled with wonder, beauty, awe and excitement, pure in emotional expression wanting to be loved and feel safe. These are basic human needs.

Yet I abused this honourable position many times. They were often disciplined through punishment, shamed and by withholding the things they needed most – compassion, love and understanding. Instead of learning through their own lived experience, with the freedom to explore themselves, they were being reprimanded instead. My responses were clouded through the lenses of my own trauma.

I have struggled with whether to share my experience so openly here. I have found that people are often too afraid of sharing experiences where shame and guilt take centrestage. It can be very confronting, stirring the fear of judgement within them. Also, acting as a reminder at times of how forgiveness and compassion seem so far away. Through sharing my stories, I acknowledge the impact it has and will continue to have upon myself and others. Giving my experiences a voice allows me to move through the emotions to a state of acceptance and grace. I breathe in forgiveness to any areas I may not have acknowledged when guilt still holds on so tightly. It took me meeting my edge to gain awareness of my actions and the impact on myself and others, this elicited the change I wasn't aware I was seeking at the time.

There were two defining events, both impacting my life choices I had made. Both introducing me to my passion for trauma and the effects of unresolved emotional events stored deep within the subconscious playing out in unhealthy, unsupportive and damaging ways. An intervention occurred where I became attuned to my conscious choices changing my entire life's trajectory.

I wish to share one of my lowest points – a life-changing moment of profoundly understanding the depth of the saying, 'Hurt people, hurt people.' Knowing what I know now, it doesn't have to be that way.

I was very clever at hiding my behaviours, thoughts, and feelings from others, and only letting people see what I wanted them to see – concealing parts of myself because it was easier and safer that way. As is often the case, I had no idea how I'd gotten to the point of explosion. On this particular day, it all came to a head.

Blinding rage ran through me, overriding my sensors. I didn't know how to make it all stop. Everything was so loud and I was yelling uncontrollably, my body shaking as I reached a point of explosion. I remember grabbing my child's wrist tightly, thinking, *I could literally hurt my child right now, I could do some serious damage.* I was struggling with my demons, willing myself to release their wrists. I was so scared that I didn't know what to do if I didn't. Fear was rising rapidly inside of me as my need for destruction was strong. I wanted it all to stop. It felt like it wasn't even me; I didn't recognise this person at that moment. I could see the tears forming in their eyes, how scared they were, cowering away from my great force.

I was the person who was supposed to love them, in a position of trust to make them feel safe – and my child was frozen in terror, just as I had done all those years beforehand. I remember a strange out-of-body experience, feeling detached from the situation for those few moments as I viewed what was happening from a point above. It was as if someone had pushed pause at this particular scene. I felt something overriding me; an intervention occurred. I saw myself standing there feeling so lost and trapped in my body, screaming out for help and change. It was very surreal as I felt a deep compassion, love and understanding wash over me. When I came back to the moment, I let go of their wrists and remembered yelling, "Run, run from Mummy."

I felt it all tumbling down in that moment as I turned around, grabbing hold of the benchtop tightly. I did not intend to let go as I was so scared of what I would do if I did. I didn't know if I'd be able to stop a second time around – reminding myself to breathe and hold on repeatedly until the intensity of these emotions passed. I felt so much fear of meeting my edge that day. So much regret, shame, anger, torment, and guilt welled up and through me. I let the tears fall freely for the first time, with no energy nor want to brush them aside.

I had put so many barriers up in my life suppressing what should have come to the surface a long time ago, but I kept ignoring the signs. At that moment, I knew that I couldn't continue this way; I couldn't be this person anymore. This was not the mother I wanted to be, this was not the role model I wanted to be for my children.

Something shifted in me that day; the fear of being at the edge and the blinding destructiveness I felt coursing through my veins. It wasn't okay for me to not deal with my past hurts. I had to address them, so that my past hurts wouldn't become their present hurts.

Memories started flooding back of past events that I had buried deep. I remember in my late teens, a life-altering moment where I had something taken from me, my innocence. I felt helpless, laying there as I felt my senses shut down. Mentally, I had taken myself somewhere else as a way to escape. Imagining it was being done to my physical body and it would not affect who I was inside. I couldn't speak, move nor fight back in those moments. Praying to God to let it be done. Let it be over with. Just let it be finished. Afterwards, I lay there silently in total darkness, trying to comprehend what had happened, not even having the coping skills to understand. I felt so dirty, numb, guilty, and I was in pain.

Deciding to keep it to myself, I had no idea how this would affect other decisions ongoing in my life. I chose not to reach out to those who loved me or could support me, too ashamed to give it a voice. I feared not being believed and shamed further. It was easier to ignore it; the teasing and words of torment I'd hear afterwards, each insult a reminder of being paralysed with fear and hardening my heart. When I needed a voice to fight back, there was none to be found. I would freeze instead.

I became reckless, turning to self-harm to break through the numbness, wanting to feel something again, anything at all, either physically or emotionally. It continued to play out in different patterns throughout my life, my behaviour changes, and my choices. I found it incredibly difficult to trust people besides a chosen few; to open up and show them a part of me, it all felt too vulnerable. Feeling like I was always on guard, needing to feel like I was protecting myself from being hurt. I'd control different aspects of my life because I felt that everything felt too shaky and unfamiliar when I didn't, and I wasn't ready for that. My self-harm abusive ways changed as I turned to drugs and alcohol. It was much easier to take something and let the responsibilities slide right away, escaping from my overthinking and control-driven mind.

After that day in the kitchen, one thing that stuck with me that my heart remembered was the look in my child's eyes, and the way their body was so rigid and trembling. The tears welling in their wide, scared eyes as a whimper escaped their quivering lips. I was so detached from their basic need for safety. There was no compassion, love and understanding as these were something I wasn't giving myself. How could I give something to someone else that I wasn't willing to recognise or accept for myself first?

I made a conscious choice that the wounds from my past would stop with me. They wouldn't become my children's issues that they would have to course-correct into their future. One thing I've heard said often is a beautiful quote by Maya Angelou – she says, "*Do the best you can until you know better. Then when you know better, do better.*"

Even though it was extremely painful at the time, I am deeply grateful now that there was a separation and a breakdown in our relationship. It was a wake-up call that I received loud and clear. Their rapid change in behaviour towards me was a reminder of the trust that I had broken, knowing I had no-one to blame but myself and not to slip back into my old ways. I had no idea of the long-term effect it would have on them, though I knew it all had to change.

Over the months that followed, we both became very aware of my words, tones, body language and actions. Whenever I raised my voice slightly, the tears would start to well, and they'd go very quiet, cowering away. On occasion, they would physically harm themselves when they couldn't or didn't know how to calm their emotions. There were moments of affection shared, though not the same as before. A trust was broken that needed time and space to repair. I was extremely thankful that my husband was there to soothe and comfort them when they needed, forming a stronger bond in the process. I could only hope for our relationship of unconditional love to return once again.

It took months to regain my child's trust again through acceptance, compassion, forgiveness and understanding. In some ways it took years, but slowly, the distance between us became less, and we navigated a new developing relationship. I needed support and guidance if a permanent change was to occur. I found a fantastic energy practitioner to work with, and I started to resolve and release negatively charged emotions stored in my physical body using tapping and other tools. Through the resolve and release process I started to understand myself and my patterns more deeply, slowly being supported to return to a state of balance. The effects were profound, and so started my healing journey and introduction to the world of energy healing. I saw hope that by working with my trauma, things would also shift for my children.

I started to listen to my intuition, going on to study extensively within this area. Letting go, finding my truth and opening my heart again has been a massive part of my path to return to wholeness. Using a combination of breathwork, EFT (Emotional Freedom Technique) and mindfulness practices, I have found myself more grounded with a greater clarity allowing my intuition to guide me. Embodied movement practices have also become a significant part of my recovery process. It was necessary to work with all aspects of how the trauma is stored, not just in the physical body but more importantly in the energy body of our subconscious. Now understanding how supporting my own system is incredibly important for lasting changes and for new ways to be established. I became softer in nature and showed more affection instead of being so inconsistent and reserved. Joy started to return as I removed the pressure I was continuously placing upon myself.

Being able to recognise these patterns starting to build and play out, well before an event occurs, has been incredibly insightful. Accessing my thought patterns, emotional intelligence and physical responses while understanding and working with bringing all of my energies back into flow. Returning to a state of homeostasis, has changed my entire way of being.

I wasn't always successful at getting it right, and more attention was required when my energies were running low – though I could understand how to reframe in the moment, bringing in acceptance, forgiveness and understanding. Over time, this has become my regular response pattern. I parent in a way that provides exploration and openness, showing vulnerability, courage, kindness and compassion. The break in our parent-child bond highlighted to me the depth of the damage that I was doing, and the need to express emotions more effectively and communicate our individual needs in a more supportive and nurturing way. Gaining a deeper understanding of myself, I now have a greater awareness of my choices. This is where my power lies, in the pauses between receiving the information and what I consciously choose my responses to be. This opportunity to reframe and create awareness brings growth and inevitably, freedom.

When my trauma was ignored and I was in emotional turmoil, it was harmful to my children, loved ones and myself. If my patterns are so ingrained with the beliefs and stories of the past, how can I encode my future differently, choosing a different path? Just because something has always been done a certain way, doesn't mean it has to remain so. No longer being aligned with many of my outdated belief systems, now was the time to create my own.

Living with unresolved trauma isn't healthy. It was reflected in everything I did until I started my pathway to recovery. I had a deep yearning for change, even when I was fearful of the outcomes. To make choices that reminded me I truly am more capable than I know myself to be, and that I can trust myself. Because I get to choose how I continue to live my life – a heart-filled one of love, intention and purpose.

Remember: Small consistent steps create lasting changes.

It takes courage to start and even more courage to continue, though it is possible to find happiness and peace within. 'Happily ever after' is not all sunshine and roses, with everyone happy. It's about how I now approach the difficulties in my life. It's being mindful, it's choosing love over fear, and every single time when shit still happens, I consciously choose to be more aware of my needs and the needs of others. I now know how I can support these changes and allow them to integrate without resisting them so much.

Through my own lived experiences, I know what became possible for me when I permitted myself to heal; when I let go of the past, making room for future possibilities available to me. The effect it's had on my family has been powerful – I've felt stronger relationships form, witnessed growth in our own children and I share a deeper connection with my husband. I've witnessed when an energetic shift occurs in one person's life, it automatically shifts the energies of those around them. This is how powerful the ripple effect of energy is. By not always needing to control, and letting go of the expectations of who I thought I needed to be, I not only have gifted myself the expansion of freedom, but my family received this treasure also.

After experiencing what's possible and feeling the joy, this is my reminder to let my heart lead the way. It led me down the path of where I am now – supporting others who yearn to break the cycle of their unre-solved trauma, find compassion, forgiveness, and open their hearts once more. No longer being afraid to meet themselves again in their fullness and creating the life they desire.

My heart always knew the way; it's about settling all of my other sensors enough to listen, and staying open and curious to its gentle, nurturing calls. Heart-centred leadership, to me, is about owning every single part of myself and allowing my soul's wisdom to guide me. When I'm aligned with what is true for me, I'm at one with myself, my surroundings and the world. I'm free to be open and curious, stepping forward with the best of myself, knowing that my best changes from day to day, moment to moment. Growth and depth of awareness come in layers, and every opportunity brings with it an insight that wasn't available previously, as I may not have been willing to see it nor open to the learnings at that moment in time.

Heart-centred leadership is about accepting the perfectly imperfect actions in any given moment. It's not always pleasant to look at one's own beliefs, actions, words and self honestly. Taking full responsibility for all choices made or not made. It is necessary to let go of what isn't in our best interests if we truly wish to continue to grow.

If there is one thing I leave this life knowing it's that one person's impact can create moments of change in other people's lives. By working with supporting the release of trauma, this change creates new pathways in this lifetime and across all generations past, present and future. Every single day we're leaving a legacy, a gift from one soul to another. Whether our gifts come from our hearts, hands or minds, we all have something incredible that is unique to us alone.

"You will have no idea what your legacy is. Your legacy is what you do every day. Your legacy is every life you've touched, every person whose life was either moved or not. It's every person you've harmed or helped, that's your legacy."
– Maya Angelou

I wish to leave you with a heartful vow of initiation to meet your soul's essence. Take a beauiful deep breath and drink in these words:

Knowing you are completely guided gives you the courage and strength to step into your fullness.

Seeing clearly with all that is open – the heart, body, mind and soul.

Hearing all that's not being said – to know, to trust.

Speaking from the heart, allow the words to wash over you, penetrating your thoughts, patiently breaking through the barriers and landing in your soul as a truth.

Feeling the joy of life's wonders and incredibly grateful for everyday miracles.

Leading with the purest of light and clearest of intentions.

Having a fierceness that knows no boundaries – taking on the darkest of storms.

Not being afraid to feel more, share more and accept the delicious opportunities for gaining deeper insights and exploring the layers of growth.

Trusting yourself and the path ahead is worth every bit of the shadows you leave behind.

"Shine so brightly that nothing can take your light away, and be the beacon for those held in darkness."

From my heart to yours, know that you are love.

I see you – I hear you – I feel you.

I witness your beauty in the journey back home to your truth.

Your glorious soul's truth.

Karen Swainson

Hey glorious souls, I'm Karen.

It's exciting to be sharing a piece of my soul-self with you. I grew up in the home of the karri trees in the picturesque town of Pemberton, located in the great South West of Western Australia. I absolutely loved my childhood and the precious time spent with family, grandparents, relatives and friends.

I mostly remember the fun and freedom of simply enjoying being a kid, growing up in a small country town where everyone knew and looked out for each other. Our family was an active part of our small local community.

A few moves and many years later, I'm now enjoying life in the beautiful Dardanup area with my beloved husband, along with our two incredible children and fur babies. I truly value my gorgeous family unit settling into the life we are creating, I am excited for what lies ahead – it feels like home.

I thoroughly enjoy connection in all its heavenly forms. From bush walking and being surrounded by nature in general, to camping, 4x4 driving, open fires, animals, being near any water source, big warm hugs and heart-filled open conversations.

Realising the importance connection plays in supporting and nurturing me, I've come to know that it gifts me presence, connecting me to my heart space and filling me with joy. It supports me in fuelling my passion about my work in the world.

As an Intuitive Intelligence trainer, advanced embodiment practitioner, spiritual companioning and EFT (emotional freedom tapping) practitioner, my work supports the release of trauma by curating an energetic safe space and creating shifts physically, cognitively, emotionally and spiritually. Through blending my many tools, life experiences and the strong guidance of my intuition, a safe compassionate container exists to raise consciousness and disrupt past patterns, so repeating cycles aren't continued, enabling new ways and patterns to be established.

I support, educate and mentor practitioners and clients in gaining a greater understanding of themselves, feeling empowered in releasing trauma more efficiently and effectively. Together we work through all of the energetic layers and put in place structures to support the transition of change, increasing their own ability to support themselves and others in a deeper way.

The words of Matt Khan ring true for me in my life; "Be the change you wish to see in this world." I will not lead others where I'm not prepared to go myself. If you would love to connect further, please do so through one of the ways below.

Always with a compassionate heart,
Karen.

Website: www.karenswainson.com
Email: connect@karenswainson.com
Facebook: www.facebook.com/karenswainson.intuitive/

Amanda Greasley

LLAMAS AND LEADERSHIP
A STRANGE ANALOGY

UNINVITED PARTY GUESTS AND NINE–YEAR–OLD CRACKERS

I jumped al-in; feet, head, butt, heart and fear first into the chance to co-author a book on heart-centred leadership. A delicious opportunity to share with the world my thoughts and demonstration of being a spiritual leader. Apparently, all my shadows thought that it was an open invitation and they followed along behind me, hard-shelled suitcases in hand, filled with all the reasons I shouldn't, can't and won't succeed.

As I signed the contract, my shadows invited themselves to the book writing party with nothing to share other than their unsolicited opinions (and all that excess baggage). No cob loaf, no stale packet of rice crackers from the back of the cupboard from 2012 and not even an $8 bottle of cheap, hangover-inducing champagne.

Uninvited, unwelcome freeloaders expressing their unsought opinions and poking at my insecurities and questioning my decisions; much like my mum did when I told her I was getting my first tattoo. Golden nuggets of soul-questioning advice were exchanged, such as, "No-one will employ you if you have a tattoo," "Only criminals and sailors get tattoos," and my absolute favourite one, "Oh Amanda, aren't you too old for this attention seeking behaviour?" All expressed as though having sovereignty over my body was a crime, punishable by disapproving looks and exile.

As the opinions, doubts and down talk of my shadow beasts (read: my ego) droned on in the background of my mind, my heart spoke in its eternal wisdom, just loud enough to be heard over the blah blah blah … *You know how to lead from your heart, you do it every single day.*

And with that, the high priestess – a welcomed guest who brought with her a chalice of ambrosia for my soul – joined the party. She is a part of me too.

Leading from the heart is trusting your heart's knowledge and its intelligence to guide you in all matters. It may not be leading a revolution, it may not look like a protest march against the demolition of the world's rainforests, nor may it look like a complete rejection of societal norms and expectations. It can be as simple and profound as viewing the world and the people in it through a lens of compassion and unwavering love.

I fought the writing of this chapter; who am I to write about heart-centred entrepreneurship? I don't work in my business; I have dreams and goals but I am not actually living them. I am an employee of a business, working in a job that I am extremely good at but have no passion for. The ethics, business practices and governmental manipulations of the industry I work in go against every one of my beliefs … but you have to make the moolah, right? Pay the mortgage, the bills, put food on the table, pay for all that stuff you purchased online to fill the ever-growing void in your life that lacks meaning and purpose.

As my internal cup of joy ran as dry as the Sahara Desert, I realised two things:

1. I have kept myself small by digging myself a debt hole deeper than the Super Pit in Kalgoorlie; and
2. I can do this!

PLAYING SMALL AND A FEAR OF COMMITMENT

If you can't afford not to work for yourself, to leave the nine-to-five job that drains your soul so much that the Grim Reaper is your co-share on the drive home, then you can't take sovereignty over your life. The saboteur in me LOVED this one!! It stemmed from imposter syndrome, a victim mentality and plain old fear. The fear that I would be solely responsible for earning my own money; that my input would equal my output. The fear that I wouldn't succeed.

I also have a huge fear of commitment, although thinking about it, it is probably more a fear of consistency. If I have my own business that needs to fund my life, the bills, holidays and at least one grande soy mocha a day then I need to show up, be brave and I need to do the work every single day, even the hard stuff. It would mean vulnerability and turning up the volume on my intuition, my heart's intelligence and doing the hard self-work that is needed to lead a rising of empowered and connected women.

How do you know if you're playing small? Ask yourself what you would do if nothing else mattered. And if you're not doing it then you're playing small.

I can hear the 'but this' and 'but that' as you rattle off a never-ending list of responsibilities – I get it, I have a burdensome list of responsibilities too – but what if … What if you could merge your wants and needs list into one, having your wants supporting your needs? What if you could have it all?

In the past when I heard similar advice, I would usually roll my eyes and keep listening to the audiobook half-heartedly but secretly hoping for a quick-fix answer to my woes. If this is you then read on.

LLAMAS AND A MINI–VAN

There is absolutely no reason why you cannot do whatever the hell it is that lights up your soul. That one thing you could talk/rant/interpretive dance about for an hour without taking a breath, and be completely oblivious to the opinions and body language of your audience. Sure, there may be some logistical challenges if you want to herd llamas in the mountains somewhere but have six kids and a mini-van to pay off, but where there is a will, there is a way.

You can have all the cake, you can eat all the cake, the cake is yours and you can do whatever you like with it.

If you're like me and have managed to dig yourself into a fiery pit of debt with a burning rope ladder as the only way out, do not despair. In fact, whatever the reason is that you are not doing what you could write, read, talk, sing and preach about, my advice is the same.

Create an exit strategy.

What do you need to do to do what you need to do? Llama herding can wait a little while longer while you're working on the roadblocks facing you now, and while you're at it, you can start working on your dream life. Hell, create several strategies and do not limit yourself. I had two exit strategies; one perfect world one (including a redundancy and chunky payout) and the other, a sleeves up, dig in approach. Do not forget about the perfect world strategy!

There is a practice that I love to do. When I feel bogged down in the mundane, when imposter syndrome comes a-knocking, I do this and it re-energises my drive to go chase my llama dreams and do the hard work.

All them business feels.

Grab a notebook, a pen and a comfortable, quiet place to sit.

Close your eyes and take a deep breath in through your nose, holding at the top of the breath and then releasing through your mouth with a sigh. As you release, let go of all the effort it has taken you to get to this moment in your day.

Do this three times.

With your eyes closed, place your hand on the centre of your chest and breathe into that space, bringing to mind images or moments that bring you a feeling of joy, appreciation, freedom or peace.

As you feel your body relax and drop deeper, bring your thoughts to that thing it is you want to do. But don't stop there – look at your whole life and how all the elements interact. Consider everything:

- *how you feel*
- *how you doing your work makes others feel*
- *how it supports your family*
- *how it creates space in your life*
- *how much money it will provide you*
- *what will you do with that money (holidays, houses, donations, scholarships, etc.)*
- *how your business will support the environment, social issues and how you will pay back your good fortune*
- *how your employees will feel working with you*
- *there are no limits – do not limit your vision regardless of what your logical brain comes in with in response*

But most importantly, how will you feel about all of these things? The feeling state is what raises your vibration. The feeling state is what will drive us to continue when it feels too hard. Forget the vision boards; it is all about the feeling state.

When you're done with your journey into your new life, slowly bring some movement back into your body, open your eyes and write everything down.

When you are short on time or finding a quiet space is actually impossible, read through your vision and remember what it feels like. It is amazing what you can create when you feel your way through it.

Side note; if you really do want to herd llamas in the mountains but have six kids, please call me – I have some ideas.

TRUST, SURRENDER AND BIG GIRL PANTIES

Happiness is nothing without fulfillment. If you're happy but unfulfilled, then happiness will be fleeting. On the other hand, happiness is also a side effect of fulfillment.

Your heart wants what it wants, and it knows how to get it. What we often neglect to do is listen to the messages. A bit like that bill you don't want to open because Lord knows where you're going to get the money to pay for it; ignore it long enough and it becomes really, really uncomfortable. When we ignore the messages from our heart (read: our intuition), life can get more than a little uncomfortable.

I don't want to get all sciencey on you so I will let you look for yourself – the HeartMath Institute has done some mind-blowing research into the intuitive nature of our heart. In fact, one study showed that the heart reacts to feeling provoking images six seconds before the images are displayed! You can read more about their work here: **www.heartmath. org/research/science-of-the-heart/intuition-research/**

It's evidence that our heart knows way more (and better) than we do.

So, when did you last listen to your heart?

I like to think of this intelligence as a firefly that flutters around in front of your face until you start to follow it down that dark, tree-lined path in the middle of a moonless night, into the woods. You see it, trust it, and surrender to it, without knowing what the result will be. Are you scared? Good! This is your growth zone, and you know that the steps you are about to take will set you on a path of change.

Consider this … You're herding your llamas and there is a severe food shortage for them. You always walk the same path but your intuition is telling you to herd your llamas through that scary-looking mountain pass. If you don't, your llamas will die. If you do, your llamas may die from the perilous journey but there also may be a bounty of pasture on the other side of the pass. Of course, if things aren't going to change, you round up your four-legged beasties and walk them through the mountain pass into Eden. Happy ending, fear conquered and rewards for your bravery reaped.

Amanda, what is it with the llamas and what on earth do llamas have to do with leading with the heart? I hear you ask. Well … who doesn't love a llama? Your life is the llamas, cruising around doing the same thing day in and day out and you are you, of course.

You are solely responsible for your life and the path it takes. Want fat and happy llamas? Then take the risk, surrender to your heart's intuition and trust. Put on your big girl panties and be brave, and tell the way you've always done it to fuck off and try something new.

INSERT MOTIVATIONAL CHAPTER HEADING HERE

We've heard them all before. Empty catchphrases like, "You can do this," and, "If you believe it, you can." Urgh. I don't know about you, but I find these cheesier than my dad's jokes over Christmas dinner, and possibly even more eye-roll inducing.

There is one motivational quote that I do find helpful, and at times, it gets me more fired up than a soccer mum on a Saturday morning. Regardless of the fear of inciting a collective eye-roll from the masses, I will share it with you:

"If not you, then who? If not now, then when?"

My general responses to this include, "Fuck yeah, why not me!!" "What the fuck am I actually waiting for?" "If [insert role model here] can be crazy famous/have million-dollar book deals/be on stage changing lives, then why can't I?" I hope that it incites a similar response within you too.

WOMEN'S LIBERATION (NOT REALLY, BUT WOMEN WILL CHANGE THE WORLD)

As I wrote my list of almost cringey 'inspirational quotes', I started to feel ranty about the current way business is performed. The company I work for in my nine-to-five (I like to refer to it as my side gig while I build the foundations of my empire) have some great values which were selected by the people who work for the company. So with a new shining set of values in hand, leadership decided we needed an imperative to cross the top of those values. The values were all about integrity, being masters of change and experts at our work, but the imperative was all about winning. We don't accept second place, we're here to win.

This imperative is deeply grained into management in the business. In my job, which includes contract negotiations, instead of a fair resolution being seen as a success (where both parties are heard and happy with the negotiations), it is seen as a failure – I should have gone in harder, argued harder and not conceded. This really, really annoys me. Why must winning always be to the detriment of someone else? Like, I get it in situations where there's a medal at stake and there can only be one first place, but in a contract negotiation, isn't an equitable and fair resolution and an improvement of our position still a win?

I am not sure if this is a general difference between men and women? The need to have one up on the other party? But this bloodlust for winning at the cost of another is why business is how it is right now.

When I dream of and consciously create my business, I make a lot of money. But that money is not for power or greed or collecting; it is so I have the resources to empower others. I will have the abundance to provide scholarships, to support causes that are dear to me, and to pay more than fair wages to my staff and reward them. My success will contribute to the success of others. And THIS is what we need to change in business. We need women to do the work they love and to offer services that women need to receive, and then the abundance and bounty from that work can be shared with those who are not able to enjoy the same freedoms or opportunities as we do.

Aside from the money, we need women to offer services that women need. Healing and empowerment, education and awareness of our bodies, reclamation of our sexuality, and the clearing of the generations of control and silencing that our ancestors, grandmothers, mothers and ourselves have experienced (and still do). I believe that having more women with power (by this I mean with money, voice and authority) will give our compassion more power. It will give our empathy, understanding and love more power, and this will heal the world!

WHY USE 3,000 WORDS WHEN YOU CAN USE 500

For those of you who got a little lost on our journey with the llamas but loved my motivational quote, here are some bits of inspiration, lessons and wisdom I have learned about leading from the heart (keeping in mind that I am trying to find that sweet spot in-between the llamas and the eye-roll inducing motivational quotes).

You are the master of your own destiny, regardless of responsibility and situation.

You can create ANYTHING, you can be ANYTHING and you can actually achieve ANYTHING.

Do not, I repeat, DO NOT sell yourself short by playing small and dreaming small. Refer to the point above. You are amazing and you have something important to do.

If you're thinking about chickening out and staying small, I ask you, "Who the fuck are you to keep your flavour of magic from the world?"

There is nothing more powerful than a woman with a mission to change the world.

You need not ask permission or forgiveness for shining your big, beautiful light wherever the hell it is needed.

Do not apologise for loving yourself, believing in yourself or honouring yourself, including your boundaries, your own space, and your own time.

Listen to your heart … she always knows what you need, and she will never lead you awry.

Empowering one woman is the beginning of a tsunami.

Act from the heart in all matters and you will be alright.

Walk the path that scares you; try a new way – this is your growth zone and you will never be the same again.

Your heart will take you on one hell of a journey. It will be joyful, fulfilling and terrifying, and you will often second-guess and wonder if you have the ability, capacity, resources and dedication to walk the path being offered. You do and you have, and you won't regret it.

Amanda Greasley

Hi, I'm Amanda Greasley, a catalyst for change in universal consciousness, a fear huntress and founder of HER Source Pty Ltd.

I am on a mission to empower women; the change makers in this world. I love women who are deeply and passionately in love with themselves, who love their bodies and claim sovereignty over their sexuality and pleasure. I hold women as they journey to live in congruence and without fear, in love and trust, and with clarity of who they are and what they want. The mothers, the witches, the warriors, the leaders, the women with a story, the women with a message, the women with love to give and the women who fight for those who cannot yet fight for themselves.

A qualified Intuitive Intelligence trainer and yoni massage practitioner, I was born in Perth, Western Australia. I have over twenty years experience in honing my skills as an energy worker, an intuitive and holder of sacred energy. I hold my clients deeply and with fierce compassion as they shift their limiting self-beliefs and fears, and fall madly in love with themselves.

Quick-witted and with no poker face, I am known for cutting through masks and illusion to illuminate the truth. I am non-judgemental and deeply compassionate. My service to the world, the universal consciousness, is to know myself, and guide my clients to know themselves as limitless, fearless and fierce. To eliminate the belief of separation in the world and to encourage the belief of oneness. To know yourself as limitless, fearless and fierce means to know yourself as God (universal consciousness), to surrender to the guidance of your intuition, to honour yourself and to work in the underworld of your subconscious, transmuting limiting beliefs and fear patterns into love. It is my service to be the demonstration of what I want the world to be. I am unafraid for you and hold you with the deepest compassion as you journey towards knowing yourself as limitless, fearless and fierce.

A devoted mother to four incredible children, I am the demonstration of an empowered woman for them all. An inspiration to my two girls and a guide to my two boys; I trust that my embodiment of the mother, the warrior, the alchemist and the priestess will show them the way to their fullest potential in life, love and spirituality.

Connect: linktr.ee/her_source_intuition

Marie Celeste Czatyrko
NEVER TOO BUSY

As a nine-year-old, my visions of playtime were not of 'setting up house' or playing with Barbie dolls. Rather these visions consisted of opening a cupboard door with a round latch to the smell of an old leather satchel which I called 'business'.

I knew nothing of SMART Goals at the time, yet I knew I was smart. Perhaps I was being transported into the future, because I would later go on to teach this tool to many women and men who were recruited into the majestic region of a successful party plan company called UndercoverWear (UCW).

S – Specific

M – Measurable

A – Attainable

R – Relevant

T – Timed

Fast forward to 1996, and I was employed at the local ANZ bank as a teller, my business card reading 'Bank Officer'. I was offered the opportunity to climb the corporate ladder – not within the bank, but within

UCW. All I had to do was recruit people to duplicate what I was doing. This involved holding four partiesin hostess' homes every week, and this would secure a regular income. As the main income earner for our family, it was vital that I secured these bookings. I also needed to introduce seven like-minded people into the business every quarter.

I had a decision to make. Stay at the bank which provided what I thought was security of income, or take a leap of faith and resign to build an empire and become an entrepreneur? I asked my guides, who I had been talking to since I was nine years old, for a sign.

My sign? A bank hold-up. A clear message had been received and my decision made.

From then on, our state manager would hold her breath with me achieving targets at the eleventh hour, and for the next twenty years I would offer the same opportunity that was offered to me, to build my empire realm.

Home life consisted of a daily routine of two children with a disability each; my eldest being blind and my youngest a type 1 diabetic which involved insulin injections four times daily. The school run, which was cross boundary, was forty minutes each way, mornings and afternoons. My husband was at home and we would role-reverse, as he put it; whilst he looked after his mother-in-law who was also living with us, I worked from home. Taking care of my mother involved understanding, patience, health care, meal preparation, transport and personal care – twenty-four-hour supervision. In hindsight, I am so grateful that I shared that time with her.

Hubby had a split shift during the day, with 7:30am to 9:30am being the first shift, and my mother loved him to bits. He would spoil her and bake her a cake every day, often leaving the kitchen before sprinkling caster sugar or preparing the icing, to come back and find a piece of cake cut out beside Mum enjoying her morning tea. She would ask him to make her a 'special' coffee, which entailed a cup of Italian percolated coffee with some Marsala liqueur to sweeten the taste. At first there was more coffee than Marsala, but as time marched on, special coffees were also drunk before bedtime and resulted in more Marsala than coffee. One would think this would knock a horse to sleep through the night, but not Mum. She had her walking stick which sounded like a drum from her bedroom to the toilet as she shuffled along. She had this obsession with flushing the toilet water; she liked the sound or was simply forgetful that she had pressed it a minimum of twenty times before, during or after her event. Hubby ended up placing a brick in the cistern so that we did not drain the Mundaring Weir of water.

She was the queen of the remote control, sitting in the lounge room on her upright chair. All consultants that came through for either one on one meetings, monthly or regional meetings, were greeted by her with nods of approval, big smiles and small talk. I remember her booking direct sales companies for parties like Tupperware, Bessemer, Nutrimetics and the Glory Box van man who would drive down our street every fortnight with laybys that all the street mums would make use of, as most had European background, and daughters were always set up for glory boxes. The community spirit in our neighbourhood was wonderful; each mum would support the other mums and attend each other's parties. They all competed with the food that was served when it was their turn to be the hostess. I learnt that they all were disciplined in budgeting to pay for their purchases in the following fortnight or month; cash was the currency known. My subconscious was taking this all in as I would later be the person who was being booked to present the parties.

I had an office in my home which displayed all my trophies, certificates, and a vision board with a picture of a grey BMW and a cleaning lady on the other half of it. I would visualise this car daily as the one I would one day drive. I did indeed qualify for that BMW and yes it was grey in colour when I was presented with it – the proven power of goal visualisation.

Our levels in the business were varied and targets were set on a regular basis. Looking back, this equated to hours of planning, motivational speaking, interviewing potential new consultants, managers and executive managers. Personal growth saw our team build their own confidence which then translated to higher achievements in sales, accolades and income. The pride that I felt when I promoted these people on their journey was enormous and the rewards were cars, travel, cash and prizes galore.

The main areas we worked on together were time management, financial budgeting and recruiting through the DISC Personality spectrum:

D – Dominance: A person in this DISC quadrant places emphasis on accomplishing results and 'seeing the big picture'. They are confident, yet sometimes blunt, outspoken and demanding.

I – Influence: Emphasis on influencing or persuading others. They tend to be enthusiastic, optimistic, open, trusting and energetic.

S – Steadiness: Cooperation, sincerity, loyalty and dependability. They tend to have calm, deliberate dispositions and do not like to be rushed.

C – Conscientiousness: Accuracy, expertise and competency. They enjoy independence, demand the details and often fear being wrong.

This is what I taught my team, which was well received, especially in understanding the art of duplication. I also worked out that people responded well to recognition, and so I invested in trophies, certificates and newsletters. I offered incentives of cash (cash was king), colour TVs, trips to Bali, fax machines, laminators and pouches, fuel vouchers and garments from the new launches. We organised fashion parades for our launches three times a year. Our yearly awards night was a gala event state-wide, and company events were usually held in the exotic places of overseas trips earned along the way in New Zealand, Fiji, New Caledonia, Bintan and Hawaii, just to name a few.

Our head office was in Sydney, NSW, and I would travel to conferences every quarter as a regional manager to bring back updates, promotions and news. UndercoverWear was the first party plan company to launch on the Australian Stock Exchange. Network marketing was usually interpreted as pyramid sales, however our company was a party plan company, not a pyramid sales scale. I would often describe it as Tupperware without the plastic.

In the 2000s we networked by communication using mostly landline phones, fax machines and face to face contact appointments. Websites cost a fortune and nobody knew if they would work back then. There was no social media, and mobile phones were just starting to appear, however they were bulky to cart around and it cost more to call a mobile than a landline number. Emails were just starting to be a way of communicating, however not many people had computers in their homes yet. Our state manager would send us reams of pages by fax handwritten and we just had to decipher what she'd written.

The best way I could measure my personal success was by word-of-mouth recommendations. My repeat business was making long life friendships with hostess' guests and consultants who would re-book me on a regular basis. Why did they re-book? Because they liked me. Something I would repeat to my consultants was, "If they don't like you, you could offer them Tasmania and a block of flats, and they still would not book with you."

Along this journey of life, our children were also learning, growing and taking in the skills needed to enjoy and adapt daily to the changes in communications. They went from a Perkins braille machine to a Eureka braille electronic keypad device, and from drawing up insulin needles to a pen dial-up injector. As the parents of a blind child, the need for extra finances at the forefront was obvious. We were getting used to advocating for their rights.

There was a music camp in Fencham, NSW, which was a chance for students to create music and experience some independence away from home, with teachers and guides travelling with them for a week of creativity and learning with peers from all over the country. To raise the funds for our children to attend, I swung into action with other parents to create an organisation called VIZHELP. We met at our homes, brainstorming to come up with ideas and make decisions on how to raise much-needed funds, as well as meet with the Minister for Education with 390 signed signatures to petition that we needed more special needs teachers in the blind arena to keep up with all the children who were at this stage on a ratio of 1:30, teachers to blind children. As there was no social media, we literally took signed forms from parents who had been approached by us one by one, and handed them to the Minister for Education at a meeting we held in Perth. Some kids did not see a braille teacher from one month to the next, or from one quarter to the next, as Western Australia had kids from up in Broome, down to Albany and across to Kalgoorlie. We managed to secure one teacher.

Funds for airfares were still needed for families who wanted to send their child to camp, and not only for kids flying out of Perth to NSW, but for those who also had to fly down to Perth first. Two sponsors came to our call-out; one was an airline company that one of the parents worked for and the other was a gentleman who had an interest in helping blind and vision-impaired children. We had raised over $3,000 and invested this amount so we could use the interest to help kids in the future. This is when the 'Heart of Gold' award was born.

One thousand dollars was to be donated first and so we asked for submissions and requests from parents. Varied requests came in, such as a family who wanted a tape recorder so that messages could be left after school and communication could be a daily welcomed change. There were also requests for fares from Geraldton to Perth to attend the NSW camp, floppy discs, braille watches, puffy pens (highlight dials), braille paper, and the list goes on.

We used the DISC profiles to delegate tasks for parents to complete, and together, everyone achieved more. These same profiles and principles from the majestic realm of my business were being transferred to the advocacy realm, and I could see that we were all in the same boat. Necessity is the mother of all invention, which to me has always meant that if you cannot find a way around it, then try through it, over it or under it. 'It' being a problem to solve, a person to help or a voice to be heard.

Drawing from experience is where the strength to share knowledge, empathy, compassion, healing and heart-centered leadership comes from. I now work at my dream job, welcoming people at the front door (when not in lockdown) or over the phone, email and texts, who are navigating the joys of national disability insurance scheme (NDIS). I liaise with head office managers, coaches, staff, clients and families who use our service provider services to make life easier and more independent. We work in a neighbourhood team module where the neighbourhood team leaders work from home for administration and meet clients and support workers in the community shared spaces. Our support workers and clients are matched together for a compatible partnership. Participants, as known by the NDIS, have choice and control; they can choose providers and support workers as per their individual plans, at least in theory. The rules have changed so much after the roll-out five years ago that the federal government needs to shake its head in shame for the heartache that some people are put through. Funds are often slashed, and the red tape is horrific, daunting and unbelievable.

The service provider organisation that I work with was started by people with disabilities for people with disabilities. Three men who started it up have gone through the NDIS process and two have their plans in place. Australia-wide, we employ, engage and support everyone who agrees to our services in the organisation, and our values align with what I believe in – respect, empowering people, creating connected communities, reflective leadership and professionalism.

As I reflect on my journey from a nine-year-old with visions and a business satchel to following my heart into the future, I know I'm exactly where I am meant to be in my journey in life right now. I have always worn my heart on my sleeve and given everything I can to make lives easier where possible. I believe this is truly how a heart-centered person rides the wave of feelings in a life full of roller-coaster rides. Being a heart-centered leader to me means listening, hearing, seeing, assessing situations and giving. I've spent my life giving my time, hearing others when spoken to, and assessing what I can give to make other people's lives easier for them, and I feel I have achieved this by opening up my heart to all the people who have been helped by me.

As you embark on your own heart-centred leadership journey, I will leave you with this final thought – travel your own path. It's the only way to be the heart-centred trail-blazer you are meant to be.

Marie Celeste Czatyrko

H i, I'm Marie Czatyrko and I live in Lockridge, Perth, Western Australia. I've been married to my wonderful husband Christopher for thirty-five years, and I'm a parent of two adult ladies with incredible abilities and needs.

I was a leader to my majestic region in the late 1990s through twenty years of being a mentor for entrepreneurs seeking a better life in direct sales leadership. I led with my heart-centred approach to personal growth, income security and friendships that are still blooming today.

'Never too busy' has been my mantra to get me through the growing years, and today, I am affectionately known as 'The Director' at reception and the first person contact at a national disability service provider company, My Supports. My Supports was started by people with a disability for people with a disability, and is where the healing begins through phone and physical contacts made. I've always been happy to help, share, give and grow through my career, and am also the convenor of VIZHELP, an organisation for parents of children who are blind/vision-impaired, as well as the founder of the 'Heart of Gold' awards.

Michelle Duke
DISCOVERING YOUR MAJICKAL INTENTIONS

"Y ou've always had the power, my dear; you just had to learn it for yourself." – Glinda the Good Witch, *The Wizard of Oz*.

We cannot comprehend what we are not ready to welcome. This has been the journey of my soul; I know I am not the only one who has been in search of their power.

What do I mean by power? The dictionary meaning of the noun 'power' is the ability to do or act; the capacity of doing or accomplishing something of political or national strength. When I speak of power it is the force that resides within us that assists us in reaching our hopes and dreams in this life. This is our inner majick and it is this majick that I speak of; power equals majick.

Somewhere along the way, we give our majick away. It is traded for safety and security and used as an exchange for love. We are quick to hand it over or give it up completely, until we finally realise that it is our majick that makes us who we are.

From this realisation we will spend much of our life combing through all the places we have scattered it, often finding it in false hope and unrequited love projects. We will call it back, bit by bit. The reunion of soul is one to rejoice at every layer.

We have been sold the story that settling is the safest and best option for a happy life, never quite reaching our fullest potential. This story is old, outdated and only ever suited those who could use this unhappiness of their peers to grow upon. We are seeing a boom in mental health awareness in the last few decades, but this isn't something that has just come about. Those that have settled and repressed their happiness are starting to burst at the seams and our mental health problems are becoming exposed at a rapid rate.

Let us go back to the beginning, according to the Bible. We are all familiar with the story of the Garden of Eden and how Adam and Eve were living a life of pure bliss, or so we are told. This story depicts the solid foundation of man ruling and woman submitting. This is the story, whether we like it or not, that has been playing out in history since its publication as truth. It has set us all up for false happiness.

We have been trying to fit this false idea for centuries and as a collective, we are becoming worse for it. The struggle to claim power over another's free will is draining the joy from both sides, the oppressor and the oppressed. We have forgotten that Eden is within ourselves. And it is time that we grow our own gardens once more.

I work with spiritual seekers assisting them to identify their self-mastery by aligning them with their inner witch. Scaffolding these women with a fierce compassion that empowers them to walk forward in their truth, claiming their majick once more and allowing them to grow their gardens to their fullest potential.

For every woman that claims her majick, it permits another to seek it out for herself. The old 'I'll have what she's having' comment made famous in the movie *When Harry Met Sally*; if we see another woman doing what she loves and it makes her sparkle, it tells us that we can do it too.

As women, we are still looking for permission. Again, this indoctrinated belief has been spoonfed to us all, men and women alike. Yet we are not the oppressed women from long ago. Currently, women are the most liberated they have been for centuries, yet the fear of stepping out of this mould keeps us settling.

In my profession I witness many women hitting brick walls at an alarming rate, often confused by the materialisation of this wall and how they feel cheated by its very existence. They are ticking all the right boxes – attending school, getting a job, partnering and starting a family, becoming the heart of the home and wearing all the hats required of them at any given moment. Multitasking is something many pride themselves on being able to achieve, yet it's not that we want to, it is that we need to.

We watched as our mothers ran the household single-handed, worked, attended the schooling commitments, sporting roles, maintained friendships and the list continues. There was never much space leftover for her to enjoy herself outside of these roles. This is what we, both men and women, are told is expected from the women in our lives.

Sigh.

The balance of being a soul-led entrepreneur and a woman who wants it all is a delicate balancing act. One that requires a deep commitment to yourself first and then to the structure and organisation that is required to keep everything flowing. Implementing this structure and ensuring others join in is key.

I have met structure with resistance, having my routine firmly planted in my mental filing cabinet where no-one else could view it. This structure worked, until it didn't. The more items placed on the to-do list in my mind, the more overwhelm began to creep in. Getting out of the habit of running life from my mental mind alone has allowed for more majick to flow into my mind.

We are creating our version of Eden and restructuring the future with every opportunity. This reconstruction pours from the very majick of being a woman. Understanding the intricate layers generated by her majick comes from the inner alchemist that resides within us. A woman is alchemy in action. Transforming everything given to her into love, when the conditions are primed. If conditions are not primed, then the chaos will befall all that surround her.

Chaos can be invaluable in placing us on the right path, so all is never lost in this pandemonium. In May of 2017, I was completing an Advanced Diploma of Functional Kinesiology, and it was my last student clinic day, the final requirement to gain my certificate. I had just switched my phone back on as I packed up my files so that I could make my way to collect my youngest children from child care before returning home.

My phone sprang to life with multiple messages from my teenage son. The voice messages were broken and incomplete, yet I managed to get the gist of what he was trying to tell me. He was in shock. Around 4pm on this Friday afternoon in May, an eighteen-year-old man driving erratically down our street lost control of his car and landed in my front bedroom window. Amazingly, no-one was hurt. Both next door to us and our house was damaged, yet this young man climbed out of the driver's side with ease.

Chaos.

That afternoon was divinely created. Had it been any other Friday afternoon, my then four-year-old daughter would have been asleep on my bed in that room while I prepared our evening meal. The only person home at the time was my eighteen-year-old son and he was in one of the back rooms of the house, initially thinking that the bang he heard was someone's letterbox being hit by a car.

Five days before this event I had set about calling in our new home. As my studies were almost complete, it felt the perfect time to focus on obtaining the dream of living on a property. I found a guided meditation online that was designed to assist you in manifesting. The suggested length of time was seven days; however in having my current home modified by a reckless driver by day five, I forgot to continue the process.

Thirteen weeks of displacement created the energy needed for change. It was not the most ideal way, however chaos always precedes change. It also reminds me of the intro to *Monkey Magic* that I watched as a child of the eighties; in the worlds, before monkey primal chaos reigned, heaven sought order, but the phoenix can only fly when its feathers are grown. In the right conditions, everything will fall into place.

Manifesting is such a buzzword in the spiritual community, almost like a gateway drug in. You start out wanting an improved lifestyle, so you find some affirmations, buy some essential oils and even a crystal or two and then, *bam!* suddenly you have your spiritual starter kit and a long list of wants. Working with women wanting more from life, I assist them in creating intentions, like manifesting with greater results.

Intentions are actions waiting to happen. All that is required from these intentions are direction. When we get clear on what it is we are drawing into our reality, these intentions are materialised at a greater rate – a slightly more advanced form of manifesting. This requires us to get real with ourselves and take the necessary steps to clear out old self-belief systems running in the background that will distort our intention.

Had I taken the time to meet and clear the subconscious fears running while I was in the process of manifesting our ideal home back in 2017, the outcome may have been less disruptive. In truth, it was as it should be, as it provided all parties with an opportunity for growth. Clarity and communication are two key factors in weaving intentions; harnessing your majick is the other.

A woman embodying her majick will hold hypnotic energy that commands attention. We will know of her arrival before she has even entered the room. It is okay to be captivated by this woman, she resides within us all. It is time that we call her home.

She occupies each of us, biding her time for when she will arise and shine her majick. She may come to us early in our life prompting us to be bold and unafraid, or she may visit off and on throughout our lives.

One thing is for sure, there will come a time when we crave to know the deeper mysteries of ourselves, and she is the one that holds us close and will not let go until we remember.

I am an extension of this embrace. Shining my majick like a beacon for those ready to discover their inner mysteries and grow their own Eden. Our world needs more soul-led women creating momentum for majickal possibilities to take up space, so that it is not only our own personal gardens in bloom, but it is the whole world benefiting from this paradigm shift.

This is where our inner witch steps in and takes centrestage, ready for action. She is the mystery and the majick and brings with her an energy that is unfuckwithable. There is a reason why history has tried hard to make us fear her. What if we retained this knowledge of the witch from birth? How would that look for those who currently benefit from keeping women oppressed? She would be an unruly woman unable to be tamed.

You will be reading this and feel that flame of the witch beginning to burn within. The desire to be untamed by others calls us. The truth is we are all born of the original woman and she is not Eve. I remember the first time I was introduced to her, I was left intoxicated by her story, so much so that I wished to call my daughter by her name. Upon telling her story to my husband and expressing the desire to name our soon-to-be-born daughter Lilith, I was met with disgust.

Why? Let me share with you her truth. Lilith was the first woman of Eden. She was Adam's equal. They spent their days together learning and exploring all that was offered to them. When it came to their sexual union, Lilith refused to submit to Adam, wanting to enjoy all that there was to be felt and expressed during their sexual encounters together. She was not a woman who was willing to live a missionary position sexual lifestyle. She knew what she wanted and was willing to speak up about getting her needs met too.

Adam did not meet this with a willingness to explore as Lilith would have hoped, and just like relationships in this modern-day, Lilith decided they needed some time apart to grow individually before returning to their union, so Lilith left Eden to find herself.

She discovered her inner majick and hung out with shapeshifters and sorcerers, alchemists and healers, doing the inner work she required to return to Adam. Was Adam doing the same soul-searching? Nope. Adam complained to God that he was left all alone with no partner to complete him. To soothe Adam, God created Eve from his rib and gave her to Adam as his gift. In doing so, Eve's fate was sealed, she had no free will, only being a partner to Adam and submitting to his desires.

When Lilith was satisfied her self-discovery had been fulfilled she was ready to return to the garden and Adam. Yet when she drew near she saw that Adam had not been working on his limiting self-beliefs as she had. Here was Adam having his every need met by Eve, who in turn was blissfully unaware that she even had a choice in her position as his partner.

Lilith was livid that Adam had chosen not to deepen into his self-mastery as she had, and instead he had applied a self-soothing bandaid in the form of another woman fashioned for his own needs. Lilith was not angry with Eve; she wished to impart knowledge to her, to allow Eve the opportunity to have free will equal to that of both Adam and Lilith.

Using her newly found skills in shapeshifting, Lilith transformed herself into a serpent and awaited Eve in the garden. We all know the rest of this story and how Eve was then blamed for the fall of Eden. And yet no-one looked to Adam, who had refused to take any action to improve himself. It was never a question as to why equality had to be worked on by only one side of the sexes and it is still an unanswered question today.

My daughter was never named Lilith. Yet her wild nature has been encouraged; all of my daughters have been encouraged to find their inner majick. And like every season I trust that the seeds planted will grow in time.

She was a little bit *Lilith*
And a little bit *Eve,*
And she was tired of people telling
Her who the fuck she should be.
~Ann Marie Eleazer~
She's Magic & Midnight Lace

Bringing the energy of Lilith, the original witch and first woman of Eden into my soul-led business is a reclamation for all women yearning to have equality. To be heard by others and be witnessed as the divine expression of the woman in the world. She is who the Bible warns us of; be careful of this she-devil for no-one can rule her. She is the wild and free expression of herself, doing as she wishes. Holding the highest intention for every woman to come home to herself as the greatest authority in her life, and in doing so teaching future generations to do the same. In doing so, we elevate both sexes to forge the sacred union of heaven on earth once more. A return to Eden.

Sacred union is the endgame. No longer are we creating division between the sexes, races or creeds; we recognise that we all offer unique attributes and together is how we rise. When we are no longer searching outside of ourselves for answers to life's questions there is a return of power. This return allows us to begin calling in our majickal intentions for the betterment of our own lives and that of the planet. After all, we are all walking each other home. And with that intention in mind, I leave you with this prayer;

Healer's Prayer
I am here only to be truly helpful.
I am here to represent She who sent me.
I do not have to worry about
What to say or what to do,
Because She who sent me will direct me.
I am content to be wherever She wishes,

Knowing She goes there with me.
I will be healed as I let Her teach me to heal.
And so it is
and
It is so.
A Course In Miracles.

Michelle Duke

I am Michelle Duke, a practising contemporary witch, working with spiritual seekers and assisting the to identify their self-mastery by aligning them with their inner witch. I have decades of experience in supporting women, pseudoscience and energy medicine, and hold an Advanced Diploma in Kinesiology as well as being a qualified Intuitive Intelligence teacher and trainer. It is my mission to create a global movement for the new paradigm witch; a woman who knows that true majick exists within her and is unafraid of leading the world in her power.

Born in the coastal city of Bunbury, Western Australia, when it was still a sleepy town, I spent many summer holidays returning there and have fond memories of my nan and pop's house where all the cousins would spend hours in the mulberry tree, being wild and free. Nature has always been my religion. Following the seasons and the ebb and flow of natural cycles anchors me into the physical world.

I'm a dedicated mother of five amazing children, leading by example, and raising children who know they are capable of achieving anything that they set their heart on, whilst being their biggest cheerleader.

A lover of life, I have always been a daydreamer and shooting star wisher and if I could reach the end of the rainbow, I would let you know what is on the other side. My school report cards continually mentioned my success if I remained focused on the task at hand. It is a testament that focus comes when it is placed upon the things that spark joy in our hearts, and that joy is my life's work made manifest.

Storytelling is a way that we can weave majick into the hearts and minds of others, weaving intentions through conscious hearts and returning to wholeness. This is my gift to the world.

Website: www.michelleduke.com
Facebook: www.facebook.com/MichelleDukeWitch/
Instagram: www.instagram.com/michelleduke.w.i.t.c.h/

Adele Hamilton

LIFE DOESN'T HAPPEN TO US, IT HAPPENS FOR US

I want you to go on an adventure with me; close your eyes.

Imagine you're a farmer. You're tired, physically exhausted. It's a struggle to put one foot in front of the other. You ache. You feel as though you have nothing left inside. Nothing to give.

Every day before you milk the cows, you go to the pantry that is in a hidden spot in the sunroom, before the kids come home from school.

You see, you hide your pantry food from the kids so it can be rationed out. You only have a $100 gift voucher to buy your food per month that you get from a donated source to feed your family from local shops. There are so many others in need. You open the secret pantry and there is nothing left to feed anyone. Not even Weet-Bix to go with the milk you're about to harvest.

You look at your husband and a tear runs down your cheek and drops to the ground, almost in slow motion. You walk out to the dairy, your feet are heavy and your stomach is rumbling. The devastation of the current drought is being felt. You milk the cows, clean up the dairy, and because three cows got out on the road through the old broken fence while you were milking (they are hungry too), you decide to walk out the dairy driveway and back down the house driveway to check up and down the road. You walk towards the front door and before you get there, there are two laundry baskets sitting at the door full of food. There is so much food and a note attached to a tea bag saying, *Sit and have a cup of tea with me and know that I am thinking of you.* With a smile of relief and tears of joy, you and your family can eat. You have food. You look at your husband and say, "let's go and cook tea." You later find out the hampers were from a retired dairy farmer's wife from South Gippsland.

A few years later you decide it's time to move away from the farm. Exhausted, ready for a less stressful life; things will be better. And then two weeks later …

Take a deep breath. Here comes the darkest day of your life!

Now I want you to imagine that over in the distance from your home and family, a pillar of smoke is reaching high into the sky and soon turns into a mushroom cloud. As the minutes pass you watch the smoke pluming, and as it rises high in the air and over your property, your fear increases. A moment later, you realise that the smoke plume is growing quickly and getting closer … extremely quickly. You look at your husband silently, knowing the concern you each have on your face. The ground turns red from the hot sun shining through the smoke-filled sky. Fear sets in.

You tell the kids we are going on a little holiday, and on this holiday we can only take the most special things that belong to us, so please go and quickly pack those special things and be quick because we don't want to be late. As they are upstairs you hear the radio saying that the fire is going through the town before you, and then suddenly there is silence. The radio tower on the nearby mountain is burning.

Your husband runs in and asks you to come outside. Meanwhile the kids are throwing their stuffed toys over the balcony of the atrium to downstairs. You and your husband stand on a mound of dirt where you both stood the night before, seeing the same vision that you were intuitively given that same night. Except this time it's VERY real, and you see the fire front backdraughting the flames into a nearby valley, sucking the remaining oxygen in the valley and then roaring back out of the valley like a dragon sending fireballs you found later 10km ahead of the fire front. You feel the heat of the flames and you feel the terror of you and your husband. You almost can't look away as it's the most incredible but terrifying sight, that you're wondering if you are really seeing it. In the flames you see the face of the devil. The heat becomes too much.

"Come on, it's time to leave," he says. You run inside shaking, breathing heavy, absolutely terrified. Hoping you haven't left it too late! "Come on kids, it's time to leave for our holiday. Out to the car please." You look around the three-storey mudbrick house that you build with your bare hands one last time. You try to take everything in … This could be the last time you see it. You look at the 'rafters' on the third storey, remembering how you held the rafter on the edge, so scared, while your husband four storeys in the air attached it somehow to the peak of the roof. "We just need to hang on like that," you say to yourself running out the door.

You are in the car, overloaded – it will be okay (six of you are in a five-seater car). You drive down the driveway and look back at the house one more time. As you're shutting the gate, a million thoughts are running through your head. One last count of the kids and you are off. You get to the end of your street, and your husband says, "Left or right? Wallan or Whittlesea?"

A rush comes over you. "LEFT, not right, I was in Ash Wednesday there!" A CFA ute speeds around the bend going what you find out later was 160km/h trying to catch the fire front. Both the driver and the passenger's head were turned to the mountain as the ute drifted over the road and around the bend.

In shock, you stop at the end of the next road and ask the firefighter where it is safe to travel and if your friends are okay who live down that road … With a shrug of his shoulders and the blank look on his face, he answers, "I don't know." A local guy drives out off the road, jumps out of his car with a horrified look on his face, eyebrows and beard singed and covered with black ash. He tells you that he has lost everything, but grabbed his neighbour's dog on the way out. You tell him to follow you. He follows you by car back to the fire station. As you walk into the Wallan fire station, the fire crew walk in saying the main street of the area you grew up in is gone.

Next thing you know you're standing in the evacuation centre staring at a board titled, *Have you seen…* It is filled with photos of your friends, whole families, people you grew up with. People you worked with, neighbours, teachers, so many people you know. You just stare. Someone walks in with a pack containing a toothbrush, toothpaste and everything you need to freshen up.

Over the next few days you walk into the newsagency, buy the local paper and sit on the park bench in the park. You open the paper and read story after story of the people who were found deceased. They are your friends, whole families, neighbours, people you worked with. A friend comes along with the paper, sits beside you silently, looks through the paper and realises the same. You sit in silence, and soon realise that there are twenty-three friends that you have lost. Your best friend has lost their house, and countless others have too. You feel so guilty that your house is still standing and that your family is safe. While everything is rushing around you, your world has TOTALLY stopped.

And somehow you need to heal … It's such a long road ahead.

Open your eyes. This is a real story. This is my story, and my family's story. We went through a drought, followed by the Black Saturday Bushfires. There are times that followed this that were a blur, and still are. But the things we really remember are the people that gave us hope when we had none left. The people that left the hamper, the people that bought the food vouchers, the people that made the packs and gave quilts, and most importantly, those people that listened and gave us hugs.

Some eight years later, I started a business. I began a whole new life that removed all of the things that were allowing me to suppress all the emotions held from the tragic circumstances eight-plus years before. I started using a natural approach to my wellness. Little did I know that this approach would feel like someone had reached deep into my subconscious and ripped out all of the emotion I had held, allowing me to feel it hard and heavy. I was paralysed for three days, head under the doona, slipping in and out of sleep. While I was asleep, I was dreaming the most vivid dreams of all the stories that I had heard – how people had died, how they had survived, and how we had managed to survive. While awake I was forced to feel (finally – after eight years of feeling numb and suppressing every emotion I had had), feeling every emotion and feeling it hard! A few days later, after several years of only being able to smell even the slightest smell of smoke, I was finally able to smell again. I was healed from PTSD.

In September 2019, an organisation was formed. I was lucky to be a founder along with another two amazing women that I am so grateful to know and work alongside. This organisation we called WANDS - Wellness Advocate Natural Disaster Support.

In the recent fires of 2019, a team of doTERRA wellness advocates, along with their families and communities, created over 25,000 emergency packs with over 17,000 being distributed to the survivors of the NSW, QLD, VIC, SA, TAS and WA fires and frontline workers. The packs contained a toothbrush, toothpaste, shampoo, conditioner, bodywash, a face washer, wipes and a tea bag in a card that said, *Sit and have a cup of tea with me and know I am thinking of you*. Vouchers were purchased from the affected areas to be given to the survivors so that it not only helped those affected but also their local businesses. The packs also contained doTERRA essential oils, to help with healing, respiratory and emotional support; the same oils that helped me heal from the PTSD that I had developed and lived with for so long. WANDS gave hope to those that had none, and we lived through the recent events with many, watching fire fronts from RFS intel. Packs were travelling on trains, planes, trucks, cars and boats. Transport companies were donating their services for the cause.

We then visited the towns affected and gave more hope and healing to the locals, letting them know that we were there and listening to their stories, as they processed the events of their darkest days and we gave them hugs. These people had also lived through drought and fires. We gave Correct-X (an amazing topical ointment that has all the powerhouse oils in it to help soothe the skin) to farmers with cows that had burnt udders. A farmer told us that the udders had cleared up within days. We visited schools and helped kids heal and gave them oils. We gave AromaTouch massages and raised almost $500 donated by visitors and gave it to the local fire captain for an improved communication system. Recently, one of the schools we visited wrote to thank us and told us that they now give AromaTouch hand massages to one another every morning before they start their day. If they see someone upset in the playground they go and grab their oils. The empowerment these kids were given to heal is incredible.

At the doTERRA online convention 2020 (online due to the COVID-19 pandemic), it was announced that Leah Guest, Petah-Jane Auckland Hall and myself, Adele Hamilton, were the recipients of the doTERRA Hope Award 2020. What an honour this was to be recognised for our efforts in bringing all the wellness advocates together, sharing in our vision of wanting emergency packs in as many households throughout Australia, so they could be the very first things offered to the evacuation centres and emergency services throughout a natural disaster. If not for the global pandemic, the Hope award would have been presented to us onstage in front of 6,500 plus wellness advocates by Emily Wright – the only female doTERRA founder, also known as the heart of doTERRA. But still the three of us rang one another and we sat still in tears, not knowing what to say. The whole of the WANDS community should be so proud of their efforts … It has been an incredible experience, and I truly hope that I have made each of my twenty-three friends proud, that their lives touched others' hearts.

However with this came an incredible feeling of unworthiness. One that I just couldn't let go of. How dare I receive the biggest award doTERRA has, that only a handful of advocates have the opportunity of receiving per decade, when I felt my worth was to lose 23 friends. I felt guilt and shame for feeling proud of our efforts; impostor syndrome had kicked in and I felt that we deserved to go through the drought and then the fires, and that we were somehow punished for the people we were. Ahh there was more healing to do! And this had to be done!

So healing it was. Mindfulness played a massive part in this journey. I learnt that life doesn't happen to us, it happens for us. It's so important to feel, as it was me suppressing my feelings that took me to my PTSD. However, I learnt not to allow it to dictate who I was. We are in control of how we feel, what we do, and making every flipping day the life we want to create. Living it today and not waiting for it to change, but making that change and choosing to live the life we want. You see, an amazing coach that I have taught me that you either get what you want or you get the lesson that you need. You never lose and you never fail. So when you feel things, allow yourself the space to feel, but give yourself a time limit (most days for me this is 5-10 minutes), and then move on. Ask yourself, what lesson have you learnt? What part did you play? Then forgive yourself and move on. Throughout this, support your body, support your emotions and know that you are held and supported and loved ALWAYS.

Today I work with individuals coaching them through their own journeys, helping them to release their feelings, as I hold support for them and give them a space to heal. They are provided with all the tools they need to move on from their own tragic events and empower them with the permission to live a life full of abundance, where they are in control of the life they want to live. It gives their worthiness back, and helps them to empower other women.

You know when you wake up and you feel like you're going to have a bad day, and suddenly one thing goes wrong and you could swear it was about to set off a whole set of dominos, as you wait for that one thing to knock everything down, one after another? Well, I have a way to change that, that I want to share with you now. I've learnt through my journey that a great morning routine can bring abundance, love and happiness into your life. All you have to do is habit stack the routine, create calm amongst the chaos and take some time for you in the mornings. Try this incredible protocol I learnt from *Advanced Oil Magic*:

1. Apply two drops of doTERRA balance blend on the soles of your feet each morning (and repeat again at night). I leave the Balance blend on my bedside table.
2. Add a drop of vetiver and rosemary to the floor of the shower and inhale whilst the steam is rising. These two oils are in my shower.
3. Dream up a storm ... Get a special notebook to dream-storm in daily. If you do this first thing in the morning, you are writing before the world demands your attention. It only takes about ten to fifteen minutes to write about what you're grateful for and what you're excited to see unfold in your life. I review what I have written before I go to bed that night.
4. I then diffuse wild orange in my diffuser (about six to eight drops) and set the diffuser for the day.
5. I then use a drop of elevation periodically throughout the day and breathe from my palms while focusing on my abundant future.

This process opens your first chakra of money and stability, grounds your energy to the present moment, opens your mind to the story of new possibilities and creates an emotional set point for gratitude in your day. You can also get out into nature and get some natural Vitamin D, which plays such an amazing role in not only grounding us but also allowing our bodies to be supported daily.

One of the most amazing things I have been taught was that in order to truly know something, you first need to learn it, and then you need to teach it. Only then will you truly know it. Time and time again this puts perspective into my everyday life and my business. It has taught me to bring people along through my journey, and it has helped me to take a step forward before I was ready, because how else was I ever going to truly know something!

So I encourage you to share your journey and find your tribe. Something you can be sure of is that people are always craving to make their life a better one, and if you are learning, doing and teaching others along the way, there are always people wanting to take the step forward on the journey that you're on right this second!

I am so grateful for the women that have come into my life; they empower me to live an amazing life every day, and their healing shows me strength and courage. I can say that I have taken all of my past hurts, healed and am now using my experience to help heal others with love, honour and respect, as I impact the world with one drop, one person and one community at a time.

Adele Hamilton

Born as an only child, I grew up empowered every day by my dad who told me several times per day for the first thirty-three years of my life that, "You can do anything you set your mind to." Little did I know how much trouble this affirmation would get me into!

Achievements were my thing, playing in state finals in netball, winning a sewing machine and an amazing pair of sewing scissors ten years later for making, designing and modelling my own garment. Travelling Australia, and looking at a mudbrick house with my husband Greg and saying, "We can do that," and we did! To do our Diploma of Agriculture together and buy a dairy farm … There was nothing we couldn't do or achieve!

Greg and I are now parents to six incredible kids, five daughters and 1 son, all who know what they want and are very determined to achieve their goals. We also have two very gorgeous granddaughters that I swear have walked on this earth before. We are very proud of each of them! Together we have lived extremely adventurous and full lives.

Today I work with individuals coaching them through their own journeys, helping them to release their feelings, as I hold support for them and give them a space to heal. They are provided with all the tools they need to move on from their own tragic events and empower them with the permission to live a life full of abundance, where they are in control of the life they want to live. It gives their worthiness back, and helps them to find who they were designed to be.

I am also now the co-creator of a membership called "elixir for life" that takes women through a journey of self-belief, giving them all the tools they need to stand in their power and live the life they were created to live. We believe an empowered woman will empower another. I am the creator of Essentially YOU which is a private container that educates my doTERRA customers and allows them to achieve empowered and limitless lives. I also run pain, anxiety and sleep studies, and am the creator of Growth Partners which provides business coaching to those wanting to pursue a business.

In addition to this, I'm also an energy healer and I would love to connect, so feel free to send me a message.

Instagram: www.instagram.com/adele_hamilton_/
Facebook: www.facebook.com/hamiltons9/
Linktree: linktr.ee/Adelehamilton
Phone: 0448171069

Kristie Inker

PHOENIX RISING

"People will forget what you said, people will forget what you did, but people will never forget how you made them feel."
– Maya Angelou

ooking across the room, I see a tall thin figure climb into the armchair and curl up into a ball, making herself smaller and smaller, so as to escape being noticed. This lively, energetic young girl who just a few minutes earlier was jumping around so full of life, now hangs her head as her eyes begin to brim with tears. The blurred noise from behind me starts to become clearer and I can hear her brother's taunting sarcastic tone coming from the other room. It takes me a minute to realise that I am in the present moment and not recounting a childhood memory; the only thing differentiating the present and the past being the rich chocolate brown of those tear-filled eyes instead of the blue-green ones I see when I look back at myself in the mirror. Everything about this moment feels eerily familiar and a sickening feeling begins to grow in the pit of my stomach.

So many thoughts flood into my brain as I feel what I perceive as anger rising in my throat. My body begins to tense up and that old friend, fight or flight, begins to show itself because we have encountered this seemingly pointless battle so many times before. As a parent, do I yell at my eldest and remind him for the umpteenth time not to pick on his sister? Do I hug my hurting child and tell her to ignore her in-house bully? Do I pick up yet another 'how to effectively parent' book and look for a way to save my sanity?

It's a dilemma I can't seem to solve … How do you get one of your children to stop spreading his own internal hurt onto another one of your children – someone he sees as a weaker, easily dominated target – when you know that looking back, he has been in that exact same place himself so many times before? And where in these 'how to parent' books do they teach you how to successfully become an adult and how to navigate parenthood when you yourself have not healed from your own childhood? It leaves you struggling as a parent because you try so hard to raise your children differently to how you were raised – whether that be the parenting style you were exposed to, the environment you lived in or the traumas you experienced – but there has been so much conditioning in your life that it's like a default setting within you that resets your way of doing or thinking all of the time. Resulting in yelling or attracting toxic people, or the million other things you swore you never wanted for your own children.

As my brain continues to bounce back and forth between, *What the hell do I do, I have tried everything,* and *Oh this feels way too familiar,* I once again hear that inner voice of mine scream over the top of it all – *THIS HAS TO STOP!* It's like hearing the ocean roar as the waves come in crashing hard against the rocks during a storm. The emotions rise up so fiercely that I feel physically ill.

I decide that these are two separate challenges that I will have to face and choose the one I feel I have the energy to deal with right now. I go over to my daughter and pull her in close for a hug, feeling her body melt into mine as she realises that she is safe – even if just for now – from the harshness of the world around her. Sometimes I am lucky and no words are needed; she just needs to know that she is loved and seen. And if I were to try and offer her words of comfort and advice when my own soul was reliving a well-known scarring feeling of constantly berating voices, then I'm not sure anything helpful would come out.

In the end, this moment with my children would not end up being a defining one where I realised I had grown up from that confused child into a heartfelt leader, nor would it be the day I had an epiphany and the universe held up a big neon sign that read, *Hey, look over here – this is the path you need to follow.* Instead, it would be one of many moments where I realised that we are all flawed as humans and that every day we need to make the decision to be better, do better and provide as much support and guidance as we can to ensure others are able to do the same for themselves. It was just another day in my life that pops up as a memory to share as I sit to write these words, and at its essence, it's a reminder of how all of those things that we may discard as unimportant minor incidents can, in fact, pile onto one another and over time, become like a scab that never gets the chance to heal and turns into an ugly scar that soon becomes a permanent piece of us that the world may choose to see.

I'd often see my younger self reflected in my daughter in so many ways and without realising it, took actions to protect her from experiencing the things that I had when I was younger. Back then, some thirty-odd years ago, my life was the only way I knew my life should be, and I took most things in my stride because that was just the way things were. It was only as my children grew that the comparisons appeared. I began to have visions of all of the things that I had missed out on when I was younger and I mourned the childhood that I didn't have. I then began to see this same mourning reflected in the eyes of other women that I met – women who had never experienced love or acceptance, and in turn, didn't know how to show it to their children, or the women who had experienced abuse and functioned in constant fear, or the women who had toxic relationships because they had never seen positive ones modelled in their lives – and I saw the need for so much healing to break the cycle that myself and others were stuck in. It was like walking around in a fog; knowing that deep down something isn't quite right, but you can't quite see what it is.

Some may perceive trauma to be a big obvious event that happens in one's life. But for those that live in a constant state of fear, low self-worth, constant self-doubt or 'fight, flight or flee', they will tell you that that is not always the case. Just as exposure to toxic chemicals may not cause obvious harm at first, the long-term results of childhood trauma, neglect or disconnect can manifest in a number of ways. I recall a single event in my childhood, which perhaps upon reflection was, in fact, a defining moment, that had a profound long-term effect on my life; my first period! I don't think it was any better or worse than what many other girls would have gone through, it is, after all, a natural act of the female human body. However, this one particular event snowballed and led me to have a poor relationship with my body, my-self worth and a complete disconnect from my feminine self. And as I picture my daughter growing up – she is on the cusp of womanhood as we speak – I wonder if she was to walk the same path now, how would it turn out for her? I imagine she would go through high school with a poor body image, she would struggle to maintain friendships due to isolation and she would become so disconnected from herself that as she went on to experience pregnancy, childbirth and motherhood, she would find herself numb to it all. She would be conditioned to see these steps only as a means to fulfilling that idealised white picket fence life, and miss out on being able to fully cherish these moments, nurturing herself whilst amazed at what she is capable of.

The day that I got my first period was definitely not my first encounter with something that would have long lasting negative effects in my life, but it is something that is at the forefront of my mind to prevent the potentially damaging personal experiences others may have, especially now that I have children of my own. I don't even recall the events in the days leading up to this defining moment of my life to tell you what the mood of our household was at the time – perhaps there was more going on in the background for others than I realised – but what has stuck with me for nearly twenty-five years is literally seeing red, and well, let's just stay that the recount in the *My Girl* movie is not far off from my own personal recollection. In response to my experience, there was a thin panty liner shoved under the toilet door and nothing more was said. There were no 'welcome to womanhood' talks, no mention of how this wasn't a taboo subject and should be an experience that we learn to perhaps not enjoy but cherish as a sign that our bodies are, in fact, healthy and doing exactly what they were designed to do. I also can't say that at that time, in my state of both physical shock and discomfort, I was in any mood to celebrate the arrival of Aunt Flo but other than the very limited 'scientific' explanations we received from our hour of education through the education system, I was pretty much left to navigate this on my own.

Only so much of this particular story is mine to tell so I cannot give you any real insight into why the environment I grew up in was so dis-connected and lacking both communication and positive encouraging support, but that, in a nutshell, is how it was. There were many words spoken that were often dripping with sarcasm and anything that asked for deep insightful answers, was for the most part, dismissed with the response of, "None of your business," or, "You don't need to know."

So, now getting back on track to how this all relates to my first period and how that thread being pulled became the unravelling for so much as a young woman. Using the resources I had available to me at the time and not having an obvious network of support, I still to this day could tell you the exact seat I was sitting in in my classroom when I bled through my uniform and had to wait for everyone to be dismissed before I could get up and leave, using my schoolbag to hide my body until I could escape to the toilets. I could tell you that my uniform for one week out of every month consisted of wearing two pairs of underwear and a jumper around my waist, while also having a toilet break during every class and using the added protection of stuffing toilet paper in my pants just in case. As you might imagine, going through this routine twelve times a year did nothing to help create a loving relationship between my future ability to bear children and my twelve-year-old self. This piled on to the already existing poor body image I had from years of sarcasm and comments about my physical appearance, and so I built up walls to hide myself from any extra ridicule and judgement. While some people might have turned into that mousey child that doesn't say much and keeps to themselves, I became that annoying third, forth or fifth wheel of a group, never really able to communicate with my peers in a positive way as this had never been the norm for me.

"Healers are spiritual warriors who have found the courage to defeat the darkness of their souls. Awakening and rising from the depths of their deepest fears, like a phoenix rising from the ashes. Reborn with a wisdom and strength that creates a light that shines bright enough to help, encourage and inspire others out of their own darkness."
– Melanie Koulouris

Looking back now, the above quote describes the path I was always going to take. Though if you had asked me even a few years ago, I would never have used the term 'healing' to describe any part of my line of work. When I left school, I entered into the corporate world and explored further education as I had pictured my success – my 'winning at life' – to be reflected in having a degree or two under my belt and earning a heap of money, which I also mistakenly thought went automatically hand in hand. I remember wanting to study to work in wildlife conservation; I'm not sure if this was just a phase that teen girls go through of wanting to save all of the fluffy, defenseless animals, or if on a more honest note it was because, up until that point in my life, my interactions with most humans had been challenging, to say the least. Animals don't come with all of that

BS, they are just out there doing their thing: eating, sleeping and keeping their species going. Anyway, I like to digress. When I started working I always seemed to gravitate towards community services. In the beginning, my wounded inner child subconsciously saw it as a means of acceptance and good karma – giving to others so that the universe would give to me in return. That probably sounds pretty selfish putting it like that but this was before I had done a lot of that inner healing and reflective work. I mean, I was really still figuring out how to be an adult at the time and was completely clueless as to how my interactions actually impacted others.

By 2008 I had been working for about eight years while solo parenting an extremely energetic little boy for five of them. I hit this massive slump one day, where my brain and my body were just like, *Nope, not doing this anymore.* I had brain fog, I was constantly tired, my moods were all over the place and my body was in pain ALL the freaking time. It felt like it had come completely out of the blue. I didn't realise it at the time but my life was toxic. The environment I was in, the relationships, the way I was caring for myself (I was still winging it at both parenting and adulting at this point). After so many tests and being dismissed by just about everyone I saw, a doctor finally decided to diagnose me with chronic fatigue and fibromyalgia. Their brilliant solution was to give me ADHD tablets to keep me alert and functioning during the day and antidepressants to help me relax and sleep at night. The response to this diagnosis from my supposed support network was like a kick in the guts. "It's all in your head," "There's nothing wrong with you," "You are just lazy," "You are making it all up," "Well don't expect any sympathy from me." It made me wake up and see the life that I was living, seeing for the first time exactly how everyone and everything around me was affecting me as a person and as a parent. I literally packed up my son and walked away from my life. It felt like the best option to detox our lives and get healthy again. I took the diagnosis with a grain of salt – like honestly, I had a five-year-old – what was I meant to do? Stay medicated twenty-four seven and live like that at twenty-four years old? Instead, I worked on doing all of the things I could at the time and learning all that I could about taking care of myself and my son holistically. This was, as they say, the turning point in my life. When the universe started to reveal its plans to me. All of these life lessons and trials that I was squirrelling away at were going to be used for something great.

There is this clear parallel between my own life experiences and the work that I now do. Upon reflection, looking back with newfound perspective, I can see that I did, in fact, make a subconscious decision to become a heart-centred leader the day that my eldest child was born. The day that my head and my heart agreed that I was no longer in this world to just survive or look after myself, but that I was here to have a positive impact on another and that I had been gifted the opportunity to support them on their journey to thriving. The time that I would noticeably start down this path would actually come years later when my wounded inner child began to reappear with my second child, as my only daughter started to grow up. This was not an act of favouritism of one child over another; the truth is that everything I have discovered on my journey has helped strengthen the relationship with all four of my children. My eldest child and I have grown up side by side as I was barely an adult when I had him – there was an enormous learning curve as I had to learn not only how to become a parent but also an adult. And my youngest has been born into a family that is simultaneously healing past wounds and creating strong foundations for the future to be handed on to the next generation. All I have ever really been able to draw on is my own experience, hence the reason why so much of my own healing was mirrored to me by my daughter. It's also why working with other women – who of course were all once young girls – is where I find my strength and connection to my work.

My personal journey has put me in a position where I can see the hurt within the greater community and I feel this pull in my gut to do whatever I can to support others to heal from their own past, so that they are not passing their wounds on to their children. I first started working with women in a mentoring capacity using modalities I had learned over the years, and this continues to grow with the addition of my other offerings. But as has happened to me so many times in my life, the universe recently came along and told me that it had other plans for me. Alongside working with women as a holistic healing coach, another passion project was born in 2021. It literally made me bolt upright in bed one hot summer night at ridiculous o'clock in the morning, when I was sleeping on a mattress in the lounge under our aircon – because we only have one aircon in our house – super relevant to my story, I know. On this particular morning, Maven Maidens was born. As it turns out, the universe can have a wicked sense of humour and the day I revealed the name for this project I became irreversibly linked to the very person who put this collaborative writing opportunity together.

The term maven means expert, genius, or person particularly skilled in their field. Deciding on the name maven was not my ego taking hold, thinking that I knew it all and could stand before others spouting off my infinite wisdom. I knew it was absolutely necessary for people to heal from their pasts so that their futures were not defined by them, but I also understood that it was just as important to support our children to create a life they themselves didn't have to heal from. Providing them with support, tools and resources while walking alongside them on their journey from girlhood to womanhood gives young girls the opportunity to become experts on themselves. It fills in the gaps where the traditional education system may be lacking in terms of self-care or boundaries, and it holds space for those who are not heard or understood by their peers or at home because they don't fit into a cookie-cutter mould.

The biggest takeaway from my life lessons over my *cough* thirty-seven years is that I was lost, I had no idea who I was as an individual, I had no idea how to speak my truth and I had no idea how to connect with my true self. I had always been the reflection of my environment, being told

I was unworthy and unimportant, whilst being chosen second or not at all. I was told that when I spoke up or questioned things that didn't feel right that I was making things up. These were the masks that I wore to embody the person that I was conditioned to believe I was. I have since become aware of these ancestral wounds that can be unknowingly passed down through the generations and it takes a lot of grit and determination to find the strength to be the one to stand up and say that it stops with me.

Maybe your story will be different, perhaps you became a leader in your own right by choice. Perhaps you had a clear plan and goal that it was the work you wanted to do, or it was not born unexpectedly from your own life experiences. But to lead from a place where you genuinely want the best outcomes for others and would do the work even if it meant your only reward was seeing that someone else benefited from your guidance – that is when you truly know you are leading from your heart and not your ego. Not to say that this type of work will push you into poverty; there are definitely endless opportunities to provide financial security for yourself and your family in many different fields. But your bank account can be as full as you like and if there is a hole in your soul that is not being filled by loving what you do, then you really are a poor soul.

If I could offer a piece of advice to anyone right now, it would be this – be prepared for a shitload of inner work to take place. When the universe throws you into a position of service to others, it can get messy. All of the ideals about love and light and holding hands and being friends with everyone you work with is a really nice instagram-filtered view on what you are about to embark on, when in reality there will be ugly crying and snot and your inner critic will become so loud that you will probably wish you had an internal mute feature. Now I don't say all of this to make you want to run for the hills, and I hope you aren't thinking, *WTF was this chick on when she wrote this?* All of that messiness is the secret sauce that makes guiding others from the heart so amazingly, unimaginably rewarding and the fuel that keeps you going when you feel like you have hit your limit. In reality, it is never about standing before others and leading them down the glorious path to their perfect life, it is about walking beside them, being completely transparent about your own journey and showing them what is possible.

So, why is it our responsibility to help others create their best life, and their best version of themselves? Because we are all impacted by the world in one way or another and it will only continue to thrive if we share our wisdom through our lived experiences with others. If we do not share our stories with the world then we deny others the opportunities to see the potential within themselves. Remember; heart-centred leaders are not those who stand before you and tell you to follow them. They are the ones who can say, "I have risen through these challenges myself – let me walk beside you and we can navigate this path together."

Kristie Inker

I'm Kristie – an unexpected leader and life-long student with an ever-evolving skill set. Upon learning to speak my truth after years of suppression, I've become a guide and mentor for others who have lost themselves or are yet to discover how amazing and worthy they truly are.

Leaving the corporate world and bringing over my existing experience and education in community services, local government and social justice, as well as human resources, health promotion and nutrition, i am now the creator of my own coaching platform – Heal Yourself, Find Yourself. I'm also the creator of the inner-child-inspired Maven Maidens which includes being a certified First Moon facilitator, as well as co-founder of Elixir for Life – a membership for women who seek empowerment and to empower others.

I incorporate many modalities, including but not limited to somatic experiencing, timeline regression and hypnotherapy, as well as cycle aware-ness, energy healing and therapeutic writing into my work. I am not only a youth mentor but also a trauma-informed feminine embodiment coach.

The focus of this work is to encourage others to heal from – but not be defined by – their past, while courageously creating a life they love by breaking the generational cycles of shame, guilt, fear and low self-worth.

Website: www.kristieinker.com.au
Instagram: www.instagram.com/kristieinker
Facebook: www.facebook.com/kristieinker1
Linktree: linktr.ee/Kristie_Inker

Laura Elizabeth
LEADER LEAD THYSELF

I 've always been a leader.

And not by choice, but by calling.

As a child I loved role-playing and make-believe. I always enjoyed taking on new character roles and performing, whether at home, at school or for amateur theatre. However, the minute I had to stand up and address a crowd as just Laura, just me … my stomach would be in knots.

Over the years of unravelling the secrets of spiritual process and understanding, I have come to learn that most often it is our greatest fears that become our biggest assets. And thus I find myself frequently asked to address large groups of people, boldly sharing insight from that authentic heart of mine. Sure, my stomach still likes to spin with butterflies to remind me that I'm stepping out of fear and into growth every single time, but I no longer allow it to hold me back.

The first lucid memory I have of stepping into leadership was my year 7 camp. We stayed at Ardroy Outdoor Education Centre near the head of Loch Goil in Loch Lomond & The Trossachs National Park, about an hour from Glasgow, Scotland. The week included team and character-building activities such as abseiling, orienteering and canoeing.

About halfway through the week, we were split into smaller groups of five or six. We were taken to the edge of Loch Goil and assigned the task of building rafts. Our group facilitator, Steve, was by far the strictest of the supervisors. He wore a big black, bushy moustache and commanded discipline when he walked into a room. Myself and my fellow students knew better than to push his boundaries.

Within these small groups we had to select a leader. We ummed and ahhed about who should or should not be in charge, before Steve stepped in and announced that he was putting me in charge.

Did I know a single thing about building rafts? Nope! As a ten-year-old girl, I was more concerned about mastering the Spice Girls' latest dance routine to perform for my parents in the lounge room, alongside my Trolls dolls and glitter hairspray (ohh the '90s!).

I remember that day thinking, "Why in the world would he make me the leader?"

But Steve wasn't looking for the person with the most knowledge and experience with tools, tying knots and uncovering washed-up wooden planks. He was looking for someone who others were naturally drawn to. Someone who knew what needed to be done and could lead a team to make it happen.

At the time, of course, I just felt happy to be chosen. But on reflection, I understand I am and always have been the person others come flying to when they are struggling or need support. I am the person who gets shit done, even when it's not always smooth sailing. And I am the person who is unafraid to take responsibility and get my hands dirty.

Fast forward six years and I was elected to the role of head girl in my final year of schooling. This time on the other side of the world in Perth, Western Australia. It was clear that leadership was something I was born to do.

Back then my focus was on maintaining the status quo and being accepted within the crowd. The good girl.

Fast forward twenty years and I baulk at the good-girl identity and instead embrace the real, raw truth and authenticity of who I really am and what lights me up. And more importantly, teaching others how to find that unique flavour of truth within themselves.

I've learned that being a leader has little to do with telling others what to do, and is all about leading by example with healthy boundaries.

The intention for me is about helping clients awaken to their own truth so that they can intuit and understand how to take action and responsibility, and know what they need to do to achieve it. We already have all the answers we need within us, and with belief, compassion, authenticity, vulnerability and integrity we can all choose to take on the leading roles in our own lives.

These are the five principles I have applied to my own life in order to be my own leading lady.

I had to divorce the damsel in distress, leave my shit behind and stop playing small.

As with any toxic relationship, my addiction to the Cinderella story was no fairytale! I had to channel my fairy godmother, put on those glass slippers and decide to never take them off! And no, I am not about to go on some tangent about finding Prince Charming (fuck that!). No-one was going to save me, I had to show up and save myself. And so can you!

After spending much of my life in the limelight, I know I was capable of making noise and creating ripples in the universe. I know that when I am aligned, people listen.

The challenge was remembering how to do it from a place that is already whole, healed, divine and abundant, in order to be able to lead by example.

Here are my five heartcentred leadership principles for tapping into your truth and success:

BELIEF

"Whether you believe you can do a thing or not, you are right."
– Henry Ford

I often hear the words brave and courageous when I expand into new horizons and take on new goals. The truth is, I rarely know how things will turn out, but I hold sacred intention and believe in myself and my abilities to achieve anything and everything.

I used to be so weighed down by limiting beliefs and habits that I'd literally end up sitting, doing nothing. I'd feel anxious at the thought of stepping out of my comfort zone and didn't know how to burst through the old stories including shame, self-worth, body image and self-confidence. These were programs running in my subconscious that I have had to work through and maintain to reprogram.

When clients come to me who are stuck in old patterns and beliefs, I can share these processes that have helped me go from striving to thriving and truly believing in the limitless potential life has to offer.

COMPASSION

This is something that comes so naturally to me when concerning others, but has been the most challenging when it comes to having compassion and grace for myself.

Whether it be friends, family or clients I have always been able to hold the safest, non-judgemental space for you to be seen, heard and held in the moment.

It took years of unlearning the belief that I was not worthy of the same. Some days, sure, I need a little reminder to go gently with myself, but it is getting less and less.

The more I approach myself with kindness and speak with forgiveness and understanding, the more I thrive. And the more I fall in love with this body, this soul and this life, the more capacity I have to love myself and others beyond condition.

It doesn't happen overnight, but setting simple goals like keeping a gratitude journal by your bed and writing down three things that bring you joy each day, or looking in the mirror and telling yourself three things that you love, are all simple and powerful tools to help you move into a space of compassion and acceptance.

Remember, leader lead thyself; until you master this within your own life, you are doing a disservice to those around you.

AUTHENTICITY

Authenticity for me is embracing all of me and allowing her to shine through every facet of this life. What you see is what you get. I am finally at peace with the fact of that others do not need to like or resonate with me in order for me to carry out my life's sacred work.

I spent years hiding and censoring the parts of me that I believed were too much, or not enough. Suspended in a space of existing, rather than sharing all of me with the people I love.

It is so freeing to radically accept and honour my truth in all of her eccentricity. To be the best version of me and serve in the best possible way in this lifetime.

When we show up authentically as ourselves, we give those around us permission to show up fully as themselves in total acceptance too. You do you, babe.

VULNERABILITY

Vulnerable leadership is a powerful ingredient when it comes to building trust and rapport with my clients. I am open, raw and honest with my own life in the hope that it helps them feel safe to be seen and heard.

I won't ever ask a client to do something that I haven't done or am not willing and prepared to do myself. Sharing both the shadow and the light of my own journey again gives others permission to feel safe to share theirs and honour where they are at in their process.

INTEGRITY

Here is a word that gets thrown around a lot in my industry. But what does it actually mean?

To me, integrity means holding yourself accountable to your values and intention. It means following through and doing what you say you are going to do and having the courage to say no to the things that are not in alignment with those values.

It means being open to being completely honest with yourself and with those around you. There are times when it truly takes courage to stand strong, but it is always, always worth it.

Remember, that what's right for you is not always what is best for someone else, and it is paramount that we, as entrepreneurs, thought leaders and visionaries do not project or imprint our beliefs onto those around us – clients, friends or family. Instead, it is our job to encourage their own truth to shine.

I believe that every single human being on this planet has the capacity to lead their own life. To honour their truth and take responsibility for their thoughts and actions, as opposed to giving away their power in fear.

When we free ourselves from the cycle of victimhood, we are saying yes to freeing ourselves from old patterns and beliefs. We are saying yes to manifesting the life we wish to lead from and the example we wish to set by maintaining those five principles (belief, compassion, authenticity, vulnerability and integrity).

Once we make this commitment, we begin to stand deeper in our truth and our power. We begin to make a difference in our own lives. We begin to lead by example and encourage those drawn to us to find that spark within themselves.

My role as a leader has certainly morphed over the years. From raft-builder extraordinaire to women's empowerment coach and all that's in-between. I have committed to continuous growth and expansion, so that I may understand myself deeper, to be a better leader.

And so it is and it is so, leader lead thyself.

Laura Elizabeth

Hi, I'm Laura Elizabeth, a trailblazing change-maker and advocate for women's empowerment. Author of *Loving Herself Whole*, *Back Yourself!*, *Wild Woman Rising*, *Rising Matriarch* and *Heartcentred Leadership*. Director at Maven Press, creatress of Kuntea, and owner of Laura Elizabeth Wellness/Erotic Maven Medicine.

I am dedicated to creating intimate experiences for conscious women ready to step into a deeper layer of understanding of themselves. I assist them to embrace and embody their sensuality, reclaim their voices and own their personal power.

I offer womb and yoni massage therapy, reiki attunements and a catalogue of workshops, education and training events online and in person with a focus on women's health.

I am also the woman behind a steadfast, handcrafted organic product range topping it's tenth year, including the risqué yoni steaming brand Kuntea for reproductive health and wellness.

My love of writing and being a keeper of women's stories has led me most recently to create Maven Press Publishing. I am delighted to be able to doula storytellers through the conception, gestation and birth of their books into the world as they step deeper into their truth as change-makers.

A naturally gifted psychic medium born on the east coast of Fife, Scotland, I immigrated to Perth, Western Australia, as a pre-teen in 1999. With two decades of experience cultivating my skills as an energy worker and holding space for clients, I offer the safest and most profoundly intimate containers for women to encounter deep transformation.

A boundary-pusher and taboo smasher, I am best known for my real, quirky and honest guidance, ensuring the deepest empathy, understanding and non-judgement. I believe it is important to keep a healthy sense of humour to stay grounded and authentic.

My service to clients is most definitely a niche I believe is the real missing link in human connection and healing for women. We are programmed to think, feel and do based on the needs of others. But we unleash our real magic when we set aside time to explore honouring, nurturing and loving ourselves back into a belief of radical acceptance and remembering our magnificence.

A passionate solo mother of three, leading by example, smashing goals and living with purpose, I hope to be a positive influence and for my own children to reach their full potential and inspire others to do the same.

I hold your hand and love you, while you remember how to love yourself.

Website: www.lauraelizabeth.com.au
            www.mavenpress.com.au
Facebook: www.facebook.com/eroticmavenmedicine
Instagram: www.instagram.com/eroticmaven_medicine
            www.instagram.com/kuntea_by_le
            www.instagram.com/mavenpress

Cherie Smith

IF I CAN DO IT, THEN SO CAN YOU

Born as Cherie Bakes on the 5 August 1975, I was always very loved. My mother, Barbara-Jean Smith, had initially begged her parents not to have to marry my father, but because being a single mother was unheard of at that time, she soon became Barbara-Jean Bakes and so the name was passed on to me as well. I was an extremely loving child and didn't understand my aloof, aggressive father, but the adult chats and the hugs that my mum provided balanced out my world. My paternal grandfather was also a massive source of love for me, but when he went out for a packet of smokes when I was around six years old, he never came back. Many, many years later he was found in a Queensland caravan car park and had died from a heart attack. Though I didn't understand at the time, I now feel a surge of respect for the man who escaped the toxicity and went off to live his best life, but not before showing me that I was indeed loveable.

I attended school after school as we moved around Tasmania, and I became quite confused by people who were mean or unloving. My first memory of trying to befriend someone in kindergarten resulted in a child spitting in my mouth. It would take me a long time to identify the limiting belief that I held that I clearly didn't deserve high-quality friends, and this was reflected in most of my friendships until I was almost forty years old.

My father left when I was eight years old and wasn't heard from until I was fifteen. I craved having a father; never really remembering or understanding that his absence was, in fact, a gift. Memories such as being thrown across a garden bed and feeling terrified as I was winded for the first time were forgotten as I built up the man that was my father in my head. There was a stepfather who loved me and my two siblings very much but I was so caught up in the illusion of my own father that I didn't really truly give him a chance. As an adult I now love that man with all my heart and much better understand the difficulties that can be faced by a blended family.

My mum finally settled on our long-term home in the government housing suburb of Rocherlea in Launceston, Tasmania, and I developed a very unhealthy interest in boys. I would be used at every opportunity, which of course cemented my limiting beliefs that men got what they wanted and left, and I developed a belief that I would be a single mother with a tribe of kids because what man would ever love me, right?

As the years went by, people would tell me that they felt better just by being in my presence. That though my words were wise, it was the actual being in my presence that soothed their souls. Despite the experiences I'd had so far and no matter where my journey would take me next, I decided to keep these words close to my heart.

At age fifteen, I started to live independently and walked straight into a violent relationship. Going back home began to feel quite painful, and so despite how much I loved my brother and sister, they were often left waiting for my presence as I missed their birthdays and unfortunately caused them some pain in their younger lives (for which has since been apologised for and forgiven). I floated around Launceston friends' flats until I developed pneumonia during a brief period of homelessness, and the doctor threatened to hospitalise me if I didn't find permanent housing. The shelter I was living in helped me to get my very own government housing unit in, ironically, the very suburb I had grown up in, and yet although the area was known for crime, violence and chaos everywhere, I took peace in the fact that my family home was always largely unaffected by this and so I took this energy into my own home.

When I was fourteen I had linked up with some nationwide youth camps and gone through the program before becoming a leader, helping to run camps, massive group sessions and weekly support groups. This meant that there was always someone in my spare room or on my couch, making my home always somewhere safe and loving to go. I attended conferences all around Australia and public speaking became really important to me. I knew that I could make a difference in this world but I just didn't know how, except by being exceptionally kind.

My first memory of how powerful I might be was upon visiting my mother. I was sitting on the front step and my brother and his best mate were walking to the top shop, and as they walked past, I shrouded my brother in light. About ten minutes later they came screaming down towards me, my brother's best friend covered in blood. As I quickly took him inside and did my best to clean him up, my brother was staring at me in awe. I nervously asked, "WHAT?" as I thought I had done something wrong.

My brother Aaron said with emotion in his voice, "What did you do?"

I replied, "What do you mean?"

To which he said, "Cherie, they were after me." Growing up, there was always someone 'after' someone and we just stayed out of it the best we could. Aaron said that they had 'had a go at him' until he could feel his sister there with him. They then decided to attack his best mate, before he finally got him out of there as quickly as he could. My friend would later give me the name, 'Widget, the world watcher', and it makes much more sense now than it ever did then.

Life back then was always payday to payday, with the concept of abundance or savings being non-existent and never a part of my life. There was very limited work in Launceston and all I had ever wanted was to work for Centrelink or Telstra, but although I applied multiple times, I never even received a response and I figured my physical address was enough to put me on the blacklist, being that it was where the town shoved their riffraff.

When my best friend moved to Phillip Island, I jumped at the chance to join her and enjoyed working at a takeaway store in the sleepy holiday town. But I still had dreams of being a government employee, and when an old friend called and said he was living in a town with plenty of jobs and beautiful scenery, I hopped on a plane to Perth, WA, where I finally landed a job with Telstra, as well as a beautiful rental and a man who wanted the same things as me. This was unheard of – a man who wanted to get married and have children? Within six weeks, we were engaged to be married and planning our first child. I don't think either of us even thought of each other as a big love, but more so someone to fulfill life purposes, and that was okay at the time.

My first child didn't come easily; years of negative pregnancy tests, operations and medications, before feeling pulled energetically into a Chinese herbalist and within three weeks we were pregnant. Two miscarriages later at nine weeks and I was ready to give up on both the relationship AND the baby dream, but I decided in my infinite wisdom, that maybe I was being punished for not being married. Although he had been asking me for years, I finally agreed to the big day. He organised everything – from the venue, to the photographer and the guest list – and on the big day, as fate would have it, I was twenty-two weeks pregnant.

When I was six days pregnant, my baby spoke to me and said, "My name is Charlotte, Mummy, and I'm a girl." The birth of Charlotte was full of unexpected triggers and I automatically became a windmill parent, ready to protect her from the world. She was such a delightful baby that being with her was an absolute joy. Within a year I was pregnant with our second child and the decision was made that I would leave work after maternity leave from our second child – a beautiful little man we named Bailey. Giving up on that lifetime dream and the significance that I felt working there was very difficult and I became quite depressed, but I just got on with it the best I could until we fell pregnant with our third child and moved to Perth from Melbourne. My husband's parents had promised a huge amount of support upon the move to Perth, but unfortunately this wasn't the case.

We didn't know the suburbs of Perth at all, and ended up obtaining a rental in Armadale. Within days, and on my birthday, we came home to an almost empty home. All we had worked so hard for had been stolen. My husband was working long hours for little pay which left me with two children under three, and over twenty weeks pregnant. The house had been robbed and I knew no-one in the state. I didn't even have my husband home to assist me when we lost our child at twenty-two weeks, as his work referred to it as a miscarriage and wouldn't allow time off.

I first learnt about our loss when I visited the local GP to get some antidepressants. At the same time, I happened to collect the ultrasound results of our baby that I hadn't bothered to collect earlier, as my first two pregnancies had been perfect. The doctor very flippantly told me that they thought the baby may have had spina bifida or down syndrome, and that I should have an amniocentesis to check that all was well. I took this all in my stride and felt safe in my knowing that any baby sent to me was fine, whether it had disabilities or not. But on the day of the amniocentesis, more and more people kept coming into the room and I had a very strange feeling come over me as though my life were about to end. The sonographer came to the end of the bed. They were only doing an ultrasound to see where it was safe to put the needle; why did she have that look on her face? "I'm sorry, Cherie, but your baby has died," she said. My whole top half involuntarily leaped forward with a giant moan of pain and I went completely numb.

What followed next was horrific, as this happened to be a Friday and they couldn't induce me until Monday, however it did mean that I had two more days with my baby. Two more days for both myself and my other two miracles to touch my tummy and let bub know how loved he was. On 17 September 2008, I gave birth to a little boy who was born sleeping, and my whole life went into darkness. We named him Kody James and an autopsy revealed that he had died of a heart attack as a direct result of down syndrome. I was angry. So sad and so angry, until the day Kody communicated with me and asked me quite gruffly why I was angry and sad. He let me know that he had made the decision to leave… to make it easier for me. He was genuinely shocked and awed at the love I felt for him and the grief I was experiencing. And that night, as I lay on the floor next to my little ones' beds, an angel placed Kody in my arms and I slept the whole night with my baby in my arms.

The doctors had given me a rubella injection and said I couldn't conceive for twelve weeks. They also advised me not to get pregnant too quickly as this could exacerbate my grief. As part of the process, I had to have a mental health check from the hospital where I'd had Kody, and upon being asked if I heard voices in my head, I was delighted to find that the psychologist was completely open to my natural gifts and it remains one of the bright points in that dark time.

Twelve weeks to the day that they gave me that injection, I became pregnant with my rainbow baby and ended up giving birth to a very healing, gorgeous little girl we named Ella-Grace.

As much as I tried, I just couldn't make a friend in Perth, and so I tried to befriend the school mums and found one solid friendship. But we were both so busy and the mum moved away so it became hard to keep in touch. I then became severely bullied by one of the other school mums and life just seemed really hard.

And so I decided it was time to go back to work and was delighted to be taken through the process to work for the tax office. Having the children in child care was difficult as they kept getting sick and Bailey suffered separation anxiety. Adding to this, I was soon surprised, yet delighted, to discover that I was pregnant with our fifth child. The experience at the tax office soon became quite distressing, and so again I had to give up my dream of being a public servant, but through this very experience I had begun to experience the types of friendships I had always dreamt of. It was here that I met my reiki master, who then helped me study reiki levels one and two, and I was soon chosen for mastery.

I started to teach reiki and access bars to others, and I was so delighted to hear that the people who were pulled to work with me all said things like, "I have been looking for a reiki master/facilitator for so long, but no one has 'felt right' until you." This confirmed my core belief that I was here to help and I was truly quite shocked to know that people loved my goofy, inappropriate humour. I'd spent years being what I believed others wanted me to be or needed me to be, and now I was able to just be myself and know that the right people would be pulled to me. Be that clients, students or friends – people were being pulled to me for all the things about myself that I used to think were wrong about me.

At the end of the day all I really wanted to do was help people, and so when I saw a competition on Facebook, of all places, to certify as a hypnotherapist, it felt like the sun was shining just for me. I wrote in my details and had the feeling that I should pull the energy of the competition through and behind me, and wait until the competition was drawn in six weeks. Well, within five minutes I received an email to say I had won and for the first time in my life, apart from my babies, I felt like everything was falling into place.

I attended the course and felt like I was relearning old skills, though I had never known them in this lifetime. I signed up to do my mastery in hypnosis, neuro linguistic programming, life coaching, Time Line Therapy and much more, and set out to create what I needed to be able to do it.

In the meantime, at home, I had been begging my husband to make me a priority and to meet my needs. Despite the fact that I would sob and sob, there was no change and I had to make the extremely difficult decision to break up my family. This, and the loss of my mother, soon found me wanting to help people even more so to live their most amazing lives. When I was finally able to travel to Queensland to complete my mastership, I had the opportunity to heal and move forward from so many limiting beliefs that I didn't even realise that I had. I hadn't realised that all my life I had believed that I was dumb because I didn't do well in school, and that I had been holding myself back so that I didn't surpass my mother's journey. The biggest lie that I was telling myself was that I wasn't good enough, despite having already developed an amazing reputation as an incredible healer and teacher. In a review by a world-renowned healer, I was even named 'The Healer of the Healers' – a title I now wear with great pride.

In this safe container of not only learning incredible new skills to help people, I also released the major wounds of my past and the limitations of my own completely incorrect limiting beliefs about myself. This experience left me with the incredible power of knowing that I was indeed here to help people live this incredible life with my main message being that, "If I could do it, then so could you." I soon returned home and began including my new skills into my client sessions and my reputation continued to grow as 'The Healer of the Healers'. I started channelling my own processes, starting with an incredibly powerful soul reset, and started training other people to hold space for clients, move them from old paradigms and to start living the lives they were meant to be living.

I continued to invest in myself, learning how to hold space to clear and heal DNA and the cellular memory, and my clair gifts started to play a much bigger part in my healings as I went from holding space to heal clients' bodies' to healing clients' souls. To then accessing past lives and attachments to other dimensions. My healings became quite huge, interactive catalysts for change.

I also intuitively learnt how to hold space for the body and the soul to actively talk to the client and assist them to move closer to their life's purpose. I started to notice clients having complete relationship and career changes after just a few sessions, but the most important thing to me that I noticed was that while they had walked in her door the first time quite lonely, depressed and confused (or all of the above), they were now living extremely happy lives because they had chosen different paths or ways of showing up in the world. In some cases it was a change in thinking, feeling or being, and in others it was a complete life overhaul – each one just as important to me as the other.

I recently helped a former client (and now friend) run an amazing retreat outside Perth, Western Australia, and it was such a huge success that we are now working towards having River Rising Retreats all around the world. My message above all others is that, "If I can do it, then so can you." If I can be raised thinking so little of myself and with very few skills or opportunities, and then find myself seeing back to back clients, running sold out-retreats and training people in my own processes, then I have absolute faith that your life's purpose is screaming out for you to live it too. It is with all of my heart that I believe that you can be all that you have ever dreamt.

Cherie Smith

Hi, I'm Cherie Smith, known as 'The Healer of the Healers', and a catalyst for dynamic positive change. I am the owner and founder of Alternative Health Australia, as well as the owner and creator of The MORPH Process; a divinely guided soul reset essential for ascension.

It is my mission in life to hold space for as many people as I possibly can to assist and empower you to move from just living the day-to-day or holding old trauma – be that in your bloodline, past lives or from this lifetime – to living a life where you KNOW you are meant to be here to live happy, whole and healed.

I use all of the clair gifts coupled with reiki mastership, hypnosis, NLP, Time Line Therapy and a born knowing in seeing how your life can and will be, and then empowering you to get there.

I train people in reiki, access bars and The MORPH Process, and I'm the co-owner of The River Rising Retreats where delicious relaxing healing comes with ease. I'm also a very proud mother of four amazing children who astound and amaze me every day in every way.

The most exhilarating thing about what I do is seeing people walk in my door or come into a session online, feeling beaten down by life, and after some time with me I see them living happy, fulfilled lives. I have had the honour to walk alongside some of the world's most phenomenal people and I am incredibly grateful.

I am honoured to hold space and share my pure heart with you.

Helen Luxford

SHINE YOUR LIGHT
BECAUSE THE WORLD NEEDS TO SEE IT

"Who you were yesterday, is not who you are today, nor who you will be tomorrow."

– Amy K Hutchens

Can you remember a time in your life where you made a big decision and you realised that things had to change? A light bulb moment, where something just went off inside you and you knew that this was a turning point in your life? Come with me whilst I tell you about my experience.

In 2009, some would say I had the perfect life. I lived in a lovely big house, in a beautiful leafy inner-city suburb, I drove a nice car and held a senior leadership position in a growing company. Life was good.

Imagine that you are sitting next to me in my black BMW on a brisk spring morning as I'm driving to work. It is a beautiful day with blue skies, wispy clouds with just a hint of a breeze pushing them along and the sun is shining brightly.

I am driving along a main road with a tramline in the middle. As the tram stops, I see people getting on and off and hear the delight in their voices as they chatter and laugh. You can see, hear and feel the joy in the world on this gorgeous sunny day.

Yet this is a vast contrast to how I am feeling inside!

As I get closer to work, the knot in my stomach grows bigger and bigger, my heart begins to race and the tension in my arms builds as I grip the steering wheel tighter and tighter. I turn the last corner and drive up the narrow, cobbled laneway to enter the parking lot behind the office. I gather my things and enter the office through the back door feeling apprehensive of what today will bring.

It is an older building with two offices immediately on each side as you enter. There is a long hallway that leads from the back to the front and I can see the front security door hasn't been opened yet. Walking up the hall you enter the small kitchen fitted with beige laminate benchtops, a white fridge, kettle and a small rectangular table with four chairs, that don't get used very often.

Further down the hall there are toilets on the left and offices on both sides. Continuing along the hall I reach my office and search for the key. I hear the back door open and feel the breeze as I glance up to see *him* step through the door.

He waltzes in with a big grin saying, "Good morning," to those in the offices and I feel this anger rise in me at his false joviality, and for the first time I notice how remarkably unremarkable he is and I wonder to myself why I've not noticed this before. He reminds me of the character in *The Wolf of Wall Street* – all he cares about is money.

He marches up the corridor, with his leather computer bag in his left hand and takeaway coffee in his right. As he approaches, it seems as if time has slowed, and with each step he takes I feel the tension building in my body and his presence is making me shake as I fumble to find my key.

I can tell by how his stride has quickened that he wants something. I glance up as he nears, to see an unhappy face staring directly at me. I quickly look away, still searching for the key.

I just want to shrink and disappear, for the earth to open up and take me. I don't want to have to face him again today, I feel that I just can't. I want to run away and not have to talk to him, but he's coming quickly, closer and closer, and before I know it, his voice beams out in a firm, accusing manner and says, "You're late," so loudly that others can hear.

I immediately feel guilty, ashamed, and then I feel my blood starting to boil and I reply: "What do you mean?"

"You're late!"

"Ummm … (looking at my watch), "No, I'm not, my actual start time isn't for another twenty minutes!"

"Yes, but you're always in by seven."

"Yes, but my official start is 8:30."

He says angrily, "Well, you haven't answered my email."

"What email?" I make a point of responding to his emails immediately, even if only to acknowledge them, and I hadn't seen an email from him since I checked my emails at 9pm the night before.

"The one I sent yesterday! You haven't responded to it and I need an answer!"

Still stumbling to get the key in the lock, I reply in almost a whisper, "I haven't seen it yet; I'll look at it straight away and get back to you."

"I need an answer this morning!" he replies, and then storms off.

As I open my door I hear his footsteps in the distance striding up the stairs to his office.

I slowly step in and close the door behind me, which is something I don't normally do. I feel defeated; I can't see the point in carrying on. I'm unsettled, lost, unsure, upset and flustered. I turn on my computer and see the email he'd sent 'yesterday' … He had sent it at 10:20pm the night before and expected an answer by 8am today!

As I sit staring at my screen, looking at the time on the email, I feel uncontrollable emotions coming up inside – you know that feeling in your stomach, your body temperature changing, the emotions building and building – and now tears are welling in my eyes.

As a tear escapes and rolls down my face, I let out a small sob, grab a tissue and I think to myself, *Thank God I shut my office door – I can't let anyone see me like this, I need to compose myself and get on with it.* As I consider how I'm going to do so, I wonder how I got here; how did I get to this point? I know I'm a strong, confident individual, but even as I think this, my inner critic is saying to me *not anymore, you're weak, you failed.*

I'm working twelve- to fourteen-hour days and weekends, and the more I do, the more he expects. I reflect on the many conversations I've had with him about his expectations, his approach and how his leadership team is burning out. And I now realise I'm also talking about myself! I'm burning out – actually, I'm burnt out.

But what can I do? I can't leave this job; it pays well, we have a mortgage, I've got a young team that I've promised to develop and help them reach their goals. And what about the rest of the organisation? My job as head of HR is to create an environment where staff can flourish and I am a strong believer in that. However, this is not a good environment.

But what if I stay? I'm already unwell; I'm tired, angry, sad, uncertain, I'm finding it hard to concentrate and I'm becoming forgetful. I'm vacillating with my options – do I stay or do I go? There's so many reasons as to why I should stay … What would you do?

I sit here sobbing gently, wiping the tears from my face, staring at that email, thinking about what I've done to get into this state. I'm stuck and don't know what to do. He has changed. The organisation has changed. They no longer value staff and are now so focused on profit that they've forgotten about the people. The company is growing and we have a huge project to deliver but the unrealistic expectations for this to be delivered on top of our normal jobs is just too much. It's not achievable and that's why things are slipping, deadlines are not being met and senior staff are getting ill. The more I explain that we need additional resourcing, or that deadlines need adjusting, the more he pushes it away. The project progresses and his expectations continue to rise, and the harder everyone works, the higher his expectations rise, and as I ponder this, I have a massive realisation.

It hit me like a shot! It jolted me because it was so clear. At this moment, right now, I've had an epiphany. This is never going to stop! He is not going to change and I can't do this anymore. I have a choice! We all have choices – I now know what I need to do. I need to take back control and remove myself from this situation.

In making this decision I feel a weight immediately lift from my shoulders, I physically sit straighter and begin typing my resignation letter and I know that this is the right thing to do. Whilst walking to the printer I feel guilty as I chat to my colleagues; guilty for leaving them behind in this awful situation, but I know this is the right decision for me.

Letter in hand, I walk up the blue carpet stairs ready to confront him and end this. I head towards David's office (he is the managing director) and in walking up those stairs, I'm certain in my decision.

I pause in the open doorway, seeing an empty coffee cup and paperwork scattered on his desk and I notice a frown on his forehead as he focuses on his screen, his head down typing away. I knock, *tap-tap-tap* on the open door to get his attention. He looks up from his laptop and gestures with his hand for me to come sit in the black chair opposite him.

As I sit down, he starts asking me about the email and I interrupt. He is taken aback because no-one interrupts him. I tell him there's something I need to say. He sits in stunned silence as I explain tha-t the company has changed and my values are no longer aligned. I tell him I can't continue to work in an environment like this and I'm resigning today. He looks at me in disbelief and shock. I am a hard worker, I never say no, I do whatever he asks because it's in the best interest of the company – but not anymore. Not when what he is asking is doing more harm than good. I won't be part of this any longer.

The relief I feel as I walk back down those stairs is amazing. I tell my colleagues and apologise for leaving them and they are gracious and understanding. I know that this action has fixed things for me and that I'm going to be okay; or so I thought.

Driving home, I reflect on the day. And whilst I feel relief, I still have anxious feelings inside me that are not going away; they are not dissipating like I thought they would and I don't understand why. I think to myself, *It will get better over the next few days.* But it doesn't. I'm still waking in the middle of the night in a sweat, my mood swings remain and I go from happy to distraught, crying or yelling in seconds, and for no reason.

My husband is worried and gently sits me down on the sofa for a chat. We discuss my state, the way I'm behaving, how unhappy I am and that I'm either angry or sad most of the time. He suggests I go to the doctor and I start crying and realise that as supportive as he is, I need professional help to get through this.

I go to the doctor and break down in tears, sobbing uncontrollably as I sit in his office apologising. He diagnoses me as depressed, prescribes medication and signs me off work for two weeks.

I have mixed feelings about this diagnosis. I'm relieved to be signed off for two weeks, which means I don't have to go back to that workplace again. But on the other hand, I feel weak and frail that I can't hold it together and that I've had to resort to medication to help me. I feel guilty, ashamed, lost.

I realise that I'm broken and need to take time for myself, so I decide to have a few weeks to resettle and reconnect with myself and nature. As I adjust to not working, I'm now getting up at a normal time and filling my days with activities that energise me. I'm slowing down, reading, walking, having coffee, sitting in nature and rebalancing myself. And six weeks later, my search for work begins and I am employed again within a week.

"It doesn't matter if you fall down; everyone does. What matters is what you do next. You either stay down or rise up again. That's what determines your strength."
– Nadine Sadaka Boulos

My story is just one example of bad leadership, but it's important to remember that bad leadership doesn't just stop with the business. It has an effect on you and a ripple effect on those close to you and your community.

After this experience, I went on to focus on leadership development and worked with new leaders, right up to executives. When I gained my first coaching qualification, I knew that I had found what I was meant to do; through coaching, I can help others and I love it.

I applied myself using the tools that I had learnt and they worked. They helped my clients, and I continued to develop and complete various certifications and qualifications in leadership, coaching and hypnotherapy. In doing so, I've had to look inside, deep inside, and one doesn't know how deep that is until one starts to do the work. During these trainings I experienced tremendous personal growth and realised that we all have a part in what happens in our lives. Upon reflection, I now understand what happened at that awful job.

Our values and 'worth' are formed deep inside us when we are young, so the environment in which we are raised hugely influences us as adults. There will be 'moments' in your life that you may or may not remember that have influenced how you see, think, hear and live in the world today. These moments can be positive or negative. You may have been praised as a child for dancing, and you grew up freely expressing yourself through dance. Or you may have been told that you 'can't hold a beat' or that 'you're an awful dancer' and you were laughed at, and now you won't dance, even though you love music and hold the beat beautifully. Our beliefs and values influence the way we perceive ourselves, form our identity and how we interact with our world. This is true for all of us.

I grew up in a loving family, the youngest of five. At some point I worked out that if I helped others, I got attention. My family calls me, 'the fixer', and I love that because they know that they can rely on me whenever they need anything. But how this has played out for me in my life is that I became a 'rescuer' in all areas of my life. Looking back, I stayed in that awful job because I wanted to 'fix it'. I want to make things better.

Instead, I let my ego and my desire to achieve get in the way and I compromised on my values because I wanted to contribute to making the business successful. I let my values fall away for myself and others, because I was fixated on 'fixing it'. This state manifested physically because I'd lost alignment with my true self, my heart and soul. It doesn't matter how clever you are, if you're not true to yourself, you will know it inside.

Whilst in another job, I was talking with my mentor about my team and the challenges they were facing and how I was going to help them avoid issues I'd experienced. He told me that I had to metaphorically 'let them fall over' so that they could learn. This didn't sit well with me and I replied, "Oh, I see they need to fall to learn and then I can pick them up." He then told me I couldn't pick them up once they'd fallen. My mouth literally dropped open when he said this and I argued that if I'd let them fall, then it's my responsibility to pick them back up.

His response was, "If you pick them up every time they fall, how will they learn to get up on their own?" This was a big learning moment for me. My habit was to tell them how I'd solve problems, and not let them navigate it on their own.

My natural disposition is to help others and this will never change. What will change is how I go about it. Whether you are a leader of family, friends, community or work, think about how you engage with your tribe. Do you rescue or fix things for them or do you lead and teach them? Do you give them a fish or do you teach them to fish? I was giving away a lot of fish and I needed to start teaching people to fish, as I was exhausted because I wasn't leading myself first.

To be a heartcentred leader you need to discover who you are; to really 'know thyself', to understand and be comfortable with what truly matters to you. Our beliefs and values are deeply ingrained and sometimes we're not aware of how much they impact our decision-making. Getting to the heart of who we are and why we hold these beliefs and values can be daunting, but to peel back the layers and reveal them is important and life-changing.

Understanding, loving and leading yourself first is the beginning for you to learn how to shine your light. This was hard for me, and to be honest, I think it's hard for most people. Looking deep inside, discovering the wounds that are there from your past, your childhood, past generations (look up epigenetics for more information on that) is hard, but so essential in order to grow and transform into the butterfly that is inside us all.

Being heart-centred means coming from a 'centred' place – not from an ego-state or from a state of wanting. When you can love and lead yourself, you are then able to lead others from your heart, with love, honesty, openness and kindness.

We all have a reason for being on this earth, but for many they get caught up in life and the environment around them. They *want* to do what they know they should, but they're afraid if they show their true self and step into their true power, that those close to them will call them selfish, they will judge, ridicule, or worse, will move away from them. So we play 'not to lose' – we dabble in our greatness, step in and out of our light, but go back to hiding in the shadows because of the fear of being seen.

The universe/God/spirit has plans for you and by you reading this book, they are sending you a sign, and you can probably feel something stirring within you. "Life doesn't happen to us, it happens for us," as they say.

What's happening in your life? What signs are you receiving, and are you listening to them or blocking them? You may be holding back because you're afraid of "What if it doesn't work?" – let go of all of that and surrender to exploring where it takes you and ask yourself – *"What if it does work?"*

Let go of the past, of what has been holding you back – the fear, regret, anger, shame and resentment – and allow yourself, now, to be you. The universe will keep sending you signs until you see them. It will keep you making the same mistakes, until you learn the lesson. Embrace this wonderful being that you are and let your light shine. Get out there and 'play to win'.

*"You have to leave the city of your comfort and
go into the wilderness of your intuition.
You can't get there by bus, only by hard work and risk
and by not quite knowing what you're doing.
What you'll discover will be wonderful.
What you'll discover will be yourself."*
– Alan Alda

To develop yourself takes work – but it is so worth it. Some say that it's holding up a mirror and looking deep inside, and this is true. As you look and see things for what they are, it is an awakening. You need to feel it to heal it, and you need to heal yourself and lead yourself first.

Society conditions us and our environment can make us conform. Back in that horrible job, I allowed myself to conform and bend my values and to sway from my true self. And in doing so, I became lost and ill. But I allowed it to happen because my ego was telling me that I needed to because of the position that I held, because I'd worked so hard to get to that level and because I wanted to 'fix it'.

The key to being a heart-centred leader is self-awareness, acceptance and authenticity. Once you have that you can then lead with your heart, be true, know and live your values, and make decisions that you know in your heart and soul are the right decisions. We all have our purpose inside us and if we relax, release, surrender and let go, the universe will show you the signs to help you find yours – you just have to be ready to find it.

Stepping into heart-centred leadership is life-changing. More than ever, the world needs us to shine our light now, to build each other up, to inspire healthy relationships and to operate with grace and love. You will know when you've been in the presence of a heart-centred leader because you will remember how they made you feel.

"I've learned that people will forget what you said, people will forget what you did, but people will never forget how you made them feel."
– Maya Angelou

I have been searching for my purpose and I've found it. I am meant to spread the light around the importance of leadership, and when I look back, all the signs were there, but I wasn't awake to them. They were there all my life starting with when I was born.

My name is Helen – this means light – and I am meant to shine and light the way for a leadership awakening. To work with like-minded people, to make a difference and raise the vibration of this earth through connectedness and unity, by helping everyone become who they were meant to be and helping them shine their light. I am a work in progress and always will be. I continue to develop myself, to look inward, to grow and I am excited about where life will take me and I'm now attuned to look for the signs the universe is sending. Are you ready to discover your true self and shine your light?

Helen Luxford

Hi, I'm Helen Luxford and I'm passionate about making a difference in this world by supporting others to find their true self and to step into the life they desire. I help clients develop confidence, create the mindset they want, overcome adversity, change belief systems and support them to stand in their power for themselves, their family, community and business.

I understand the importance of leadership of self just as much as being a leader of others. I'm an authentic leader, coach and hypnotherapist and I bring confidence and support to my clients. I do this through coaching and awakening of spirit to allow my clients to recognise who they are, who they want to be and help them move forward.

I walk alongside them as they discover and explore new ways of being and become who they want to be. I have an innate ability to see and understand others which helps me create an encouraging and safe space for clients to explore and generate profound inner change and experience deep transformation.

The processes I use can unlock deep-rooted negative thought patterns and emotions and allow you to release them. With over twenty years of experience honing my skills and working with others to bring out their best, I know how to create and hold space for my clients to express themselves, process and produce the changes they are seeking.

Never being comfortable with the status quo, I'm constantly learning and developing myself to be the best I can be and am known for my loud, caring generosity of spirit. My focus is on supporting others to recognise and work towards their dreams and every modality I use with my clients; I have personally experienced.

In learning to lead myself, I've changed my inner critic from *I can't* to *how can I?* and have taught myself to catch, cancel and correct that inner voice.

The most rewarding part of my job is seeing clients arrive feeling unsure, hesitant, deflated, sad and leave feeling confident, assured, happy and ready to step forward. I'm both honoured and humbled by the work I do. If you're resonating with this, please reach out and let's see how we can work together.

Instagram:	www.instagram.com/helenluxford100/
	www.instagram.com/corporateleadershipcoaching/
Facebook:	www.facebook.com/CorpLeadCoach/
	www.facebook.com/helenluxford100
Website:	www.corporateleadershipcoaching.com.au
	www.helenluxford.com

Bonnie Collins

GO INWARD

Heart-centred leadership. These words, when strung together, emit a sense of blissful and gentle dealings; of full cups over-flowing, pouring forth and meeting needs with ease and grace.

In a practical sense, when it comes to leadership, I can only speak from my own experience, lived and observed. And the more I think about it, the entire process of business leadership is akin to creating and birthing a baby – because in a way, you are. And just like the arrival of the most precious newborn baby, the creation of a business and stepping into leadership is also not without some discomfort, growth, change, pain and more likely than not, a bit of mess.

It all starts out with a bit of fun. You have all these ideas and ideals of how it's going to be, and how good you're going to be at it. It's exciting! And then it gets a bit uncomfortable as things start to change and grow, and you too start to change. There are some adjustments to make. Fear, doubt or imposter syndrome might show up; uncertainty too as now nothing is guaranteed. *Was this a good idea?*, you ask. *Can I really be responsible for this?* But now the wheels are in motion; you've committed. There's no turning back.

The pain and the mess, akin to having a baby, will vary from person to person. Some people take all there is on offer in the way of support or to 'ease the pain', some opt to go it alone and handle things as and when they come about, and others don't have time to make or stick to a plan because once that ball is set in motion, there's no stopping it. And suddenly there you are – a wide-eyed new parent – a new business owner – a leader.

Now what?

First, the bliss bubble. "We did it – it's amazing."

Then the celebration.

The fuss.

The onset of unsolicited but well-meaning advice.

The sleepless nights.

The hours of work you don't receive a cent for.

The curve balls no one tells you about.

The heart-sinking thought that you were wrong – you can't do this …

And then all it takes is that one good moment to pull you back into the NOW and you see that it's all worth it. You repeat this cycle countless times, and in a nutshell, that's how heart centred leadership begins – especially when you're relatively new to the game.

At this point you might be wondering, why is it such a roller-coaster? I believe it's because as a heart-centred leader, you care. I mean you *really care*. I'd even go as far as to say that if you don't care about the people you are in service to, then you have no business being in service. And that caring version of YOU is the driving force at the centre of your business, just as the heart is the driving force at the centre of your body. So it's our thoughts, our vision, our intention, our values and our unique way of seeing, explaining and delivering things. It's all you. You. Are. Your. Business.

So by now I'm sure you can begin to see how your visions of a perfectly orchestrated nine to five, a beautiful work-life balance with no mum guilt, never feeling like the absent friend or partner, and a household that operates seamlessly whilst you lead a heart-centred business *were naive at best*.

It's hard work and whilst there are definitely days where I live for what I do – exuding an enthusiasm for everything and everyone where I can't wait to share what I have – there are also days I'd rather run away or stay on the couch. Is this normal? Absolutely. Does it impact your business? Yes. Because again, you are your business. So, how do you tackle the inevitable tough days?

Playing in this league can be isolating so there's a need for real friends and community who will (with love, always) be there to receive a call, give you a safe place to vent, rant, throw a tantrum if you must and then remind you of your WHY. And there will also come a time (trust me) when you'll need those same people to call you out on your shit entirely, for playing small or trying at times to not play at all.

And with that, your business becomes this collaboration of everything positive you want to offer, whilst also providing you with the opportunity to challenge your very own patterns in life, like:

How you face your patterns/habits, or don't.

How you show up, or don't.

Or how you heal and grow, or don't.

In the end, your business becomes a place of healing and development for you, just as much as it is for the people you are in service to.

Then there's the topic of boundaries – you need them. Full stop. Boundaries in a business, particularly one that is heart-centred, are crucial because your nature is to be and act in service, with love – and loving yourself first is the best example to lead with. Alongside the fact that there's generally always going to be something or someone that will be needing your attention, so you're going to need boundaries with your time, your energy, your space, your accessibility and your exchange. Any source that you give from needs a boundary – a lack of boundaries leaves you open to a lack of respect.

These days, being a leader is not about repackaging the same thing someone else has already done and getting more clients, or the clients that are left over or in your immediate area. It's not about how big you are, how well you're known or how many followers you have; it's about offering something that's of true value, that's accessible and that meets a need. Maybe it's something a little different to what's already out there or maybe it's not like anything we've ever seen before; either way, leading is about being of and acting in service with real intention behind what you do. People generally have access to whatever they want these days at the click of a button. It's no longer about 'things' – people need more than that – so heart-centred leaders need to be and offer MORE. How? It all starts with your WHY.

Because your business is an entity all on its own as well as being an extension of you, your WHY is crucial. It's the foundation – the thing you will return to time and time again that will drive you to keep going, to be more, to offer more and to serve more.

Want to uncover yours? Ask yourself – *What encounter or experience originally ignited the spark in you? Or what was lacking in your own experience that allowed you to see a need, and feel that you could meet it and contribute to being that change?*

Here is a little insight into how this unfolded for me on my journey into leadership:

My desire and my purpose has always been to help bring people back into a healthy relationship with their bodies and cultivate a space that allows for radical self-acceptance, healing and growth. This is where my passion lies. It has taken me years to understand that our bodies are really just a vehicle or a tool – they are not WHO we are. Instead, they house who we are and allow us to carry out the tasks we are actually here to do.

Sadly, when it comes to our being, so much focus has been placed on our exterior that often our interior is left wanting. But like any well-oiled relationship, the two parties need to work together for a positive outcome. Our relationships with our bodies have become a battle; it's all-out war for some and I feel that the battlefield just keeps getting bigger and bigger.

As the external offenders grow – the unrelenting stream of social media, magazines, window displays, TV advertising and more – they drive unrealistic and unhealthy body image, allowing the internal offenders room to advance also. Our inner voice is being subconsciously programmed to compare and exist in a state of lack. So much so that many people don't even know the sound of their own inner voice anymore and are consumed with the noise around them.

I completely understand that loss of self. It can be overwhelming as it is such a huge adversary to take on and my own battle scars run deep. On the one hand, I have a huge love of movement, embodiment and expression using the body as a medium, but I also have a complicated past (and still at times, present) with body image issues, eating disorders, self-love and self-acceptance.

As a Pilates instructor, barre instructor and studio owner/operator, I find myself immersed within an industry that is essentially in a position to help people live healthier, happier lives, and should be making people feel better in their own skin. Yet I see it all too often having the exact opposite effect. Health, fitness and wellness are all a part of an industry that has become grossly intertwined with toxic body image, diet culture and frankly, a whole cohort of undesirable traits.

Daily, I see comparison, body shaming, fatphobia, lies, false promises, elitist attitudes and exclusivity, just to name a few. And when you add in just how unregulated the health, fitness and wellness industry is, this allows individuals with little to no training or accountability to step in, potentially creating some dangerous situations.

So, I find myself fighting this battle, it would seem, from behind enemy lines. How do you take on an industry that has, for as long as I can recall, played on people's insecurities and made obscene amounts of money reinforcing that you are not enough unless you do, have, be or look like XYZ …? You don't. You take on your own position within that industry – and you take that battle INWARD.

You align yourself with the values you hold, and set solid and steadfast intentions for the work that you do and offer. You have hard boundaries of what you will and won't entertain within your own world and the space you provide for others. And then you get transparent with your own battles – because you lead by example. You cannot really help someone if you are in hiding.

You must also learn to trust – trust that you are not really alone. Like with all things, the pendulum can only swing so far one way before it has to start swinging back. I see this happening, I feel it happening and I have hope. It's a slow process but there are amazing humans and businesses emerging, questioning how we do things and why, and questioning is where it all begins. These questions are the very things that spark new information and change.

We know that knowledge is power, but it is only power if we can ACT on it. So for me, teaching my people the importance of how they feel is where I find I can really empower and equip individuals to be able to take action. We've all been caught in the crossfire of this body battlefield and I believe one of the first casualties was our ability to tune in and know how we actually FEEL rather than how we've been programmed to feel, or more so, how we've been programmed to respond. I see this all too often, even in basic conversation, and it goes something like this:

"Hey, how do you feel today?"

"I feel fat"

"Okay, hear me out. Fat isn't really a feeling, so how do you FEEL?

Cue crickets and wide eyes here

Their response is way too often one of shock, and simply, "I don't know." The words being used aren't even our own, so often people no longer know how they feel. They've just been convinced that they don't measure up to some ridiculous standard so they are disillusioned and treating their body as though it's failed them somehow.

Now I'm sure I'm not the first person to ever make this connection and highlight 'feeling fat', and I wish I knew who first did so I could credit them and perhaps give them a medal. But what's most important here is that we have been programmed to believe that we feel how we look, and it's a blatant lie. The language we use is so important, and the more mindful you become with your words, the more they can work for you. They lay the foundation for a great deal of our experiences.

Just like we're often told that we have to inhale here, exhale there, only do x-amount of reps or eat said number of calories – these are all options with reasoning behind them, but when applied as a blanket rule, they become just another way for us to hand over our autonomy over our own bodies, feeding into the illusion that someone else holds the key to how good or bad you get to feel within yourself.

And I've been there and done this dance many times over. The diets, working out to tick boxes or purely for aesthetics that someone else has deemed desirable, ignoring how my body actually felt, stifling my cues for hunger, ignoring that I'm full, sleep deprivation, cosmetic surgery – Yes, all of it. And none of it made me feel good long-term, because all of it had one or several layers of disconnectedness. The fads, changes and actions I was taking were not in alignment with the ever-changing life that I have and the body that I dwell in, and they weren't serving me to fulfil my purpose. I wasn't sitting with what I needed. I was forever focused on what I thought I wasn't, which allowed little room to enjoy the freedoms and fun of what I was. Moving away from this approach not only changed how I felt within, but also shaped the leader I became as well.

So much of the leader I choose to be now has been set in this knowing of what I don't want to be and what I don't want my business to be about. If you're after a quick fix, a magic pill, an easy way out or for someone to just give you the answers or change what you look like – I am not your girl. **Anyone who claims to be able to fix you is a part of the problem.**

You are not broken. You do not need fixing. You are not meant to be anyone but your unique self. Yes, you might benefit from some tools and a safe space to reconnect with yourself; a space to learn what your body is needing from you, so IT CAN SERVE YOU – because after all, that is its job – not to simply look a certain way. But this will transpire differently for everyone, there is no one size fits all.

Knowing just how individual we all are, and were intended to be, I believe that regardless of what you're offering as a leader, you need to first learn the rules or the basics in your given industry as a framework. This will allow you to bend and break them when and where necessary in a safe way. Understanding the 'why', so we can look at the 'why not' and the 'what else'. This will equip you with tools to help guide people on their own journey as opposed to a set of rules that could restrict them and their potential.

When I operate in my studio, I look far more into the energy of the people in front of me than I do at a program of nicely strung together moves. I want to know what's happening in your world, to understand what it is you've been asking of your body, so I know how to better help replenish your state of being right now and help you walk out feeling re-energised. I want to know what is going to get you through your days with ease. I want to know what you enjoy and if you don't yet know these things, I love having the honour of being entrusted along the way to helping you rediscover them.

I one hundred per cent acknowledge that the path and progress are not linear – heck, the goal will change too – probably countless times (and this is a good thing!). If we are not changing, we're not moving, and then we are stagnating. Learning to honour your body allows you to meet him/her/it where they are at and this is why statements such as 'no pain, no gain' don't really have a space in my world. Movement of your body is movement of your energy and it should be a celebration, an exploration and a release – never a punishment.

Learn to really listen to your body. Learn to know and trust yourself and what is good for you. No piece of paper, qualification, numbers of years or experience in this field will ever make me or any other practitioner more of an expert on you or your body than you are.

Your body is your gift and yours alone, and what comes from working in unison with it allows the flow of gifts that you can share with others and then your real magic can find its way out into the world.

When you as a leader continue to level up and serve, you and your clients continue to grow, and so the cycle continues onward and upward, inward and outward – all the things in all the ways. Changing only with need and purpose, and giving yourself and others permission to be exactly what they need to be in this moment.

If you are thinking of taking that step into leadership, or if you find yourself already there, you may feel a deep knowing within, or perhaps right now it's more of a niggling question. Either way, trust yourself. We all have something worth offering, and we all have a unique way that no-one else but us can deliver. We need to step inward before we can step forward; sit with your heart and yourself long enough to know your own voice above all the noise and you will succeed.

Can you do that under the banner of someone else's business? Sure, to a degree. But if that's what works for you, I highly doubt you'd be here amongst these pages. So again, I say – listen, feel, know, act and let your magic flow. Being yourself allows you to lead from the heart and heart-centred leadership is the only kind that we all really need. Now more than ever.

Bonnie Collins

Born and raised in Perth, Western Australia, I grew up feeling disconnected from my own body. Having worked for years on myself and with others, I wholeheartedly believe that the most important relationship you will ever have in your life is the one that you have with yourself. The unison between the mind and body is designed to be a beautiful thing, and something I want everyone to experience, which is why I am an advocate for positive body image, self-love, positive thinking, doing the hard work and taking ownership of your own journey.

I also know that this isn't an easy journey and we're not meant to do it alone. So no matter where you find yourself along this path, know that I am happy to meet you there with a coffee, a word of encouragement and a way to bring you back into your body, to stir up some energy and to get you feeling more at peace with yourself than at war.

I'm also a mother to one strong, amazing daughter and one of eight children myself, so caring and nurturing others is a part of my nature, alongside my honest, no-nonsense and often no-filter approach to life.

I found my ability to connect myself and others with their bodies through my own love of movement, and as a certified Pilates and barre instructor I created SWAI – a place for movement, health and happiness. Offering a space where you are invited to be seen, to be heard and to discover YOU. The heart of my work is never about finding ways to change who you are, but instead, embracing all of the different parts of you and building a relationship with each aspect, so that you can discover what sets your soul on fire and light up those around you too.

Website: www.swai.com.au
Email: bonnie@swai.com.au
Facebook: www.facebook.com/bonnie.collins.9216
www.facebook.com/movement.health.happiness
Instagram: www.instagram.com/swai_movement.health.happiness/
www.instagram.com/bon_collins/

Nikki Domeney

FROM A WHISPER TO A ROAR

A mentor once said to me, "Anyone can be a leader, all it takes is courage." My own leadership journey has not been the loud roar of a courageous lioness, but more a gentle whisper that found its roar as she learnt to embrace her authenticity and empower others through leading with her heart and head in equal measure. To me, this is what it means to lead wholeheartedly.

I've attempted to look back and reach into the pockets of my childhood memories and seek out where my leadership streaks presented themselves, and where I started to show signs of stepping out and stepping up. There was that one time as a young child after being ill, where out of refusal to take medicine with such fierceness, my mum, along with a close neighbour, held me down with determined strength to ensure I took the medicine. I recall my refusal not being out of fear of taking the medicine, but more as an act of recognition that I could in fact test the boundary of what I was told to do. Nonetheless, I lost that challenge and the medicine went swiftly down as these two grown-ups who outweighed me in strength sat on me to force-feed me the sickly syrupy medicine. I remember the look of shame on my mum's face for having to resort to such force to simply keep me safe, and how I met it with a humorous joke to put her at ease about how I sure was glad that it was both of them holding me down and not the other neighbour who was just a tad overweight! Whatever anger I'd had towards them at this point hadn't lasted long, as I recall the empathy that I felt as I looked into my mum's eyes at the time. From an early age I'd had the ability to sense what was 'going on' for those around me – picking up on their energy, feelings and thoughts – and in this case, I could sense what was going on for my mum. The need to keep me safe was far stronger for her, so in fear of me not returning to good health, she did what she felt she needed to do – apply pressure. Over time, I've come to tap into this gift of empathy and understanding and hold it closely throughout my leadership journey, including having empathy for myself, and I continue to meet people and their challenges with this desire and commitment to understand them, their fears and their motivations. However, I only really got here by learning to listen and by harnessing my own self-awareness. I had to understand my own fears and false narratives, redefine my possibilities and get clear on my own values and visions. To lead, I must accept my own vulnerabilities.

In search of another time, I recall smoking with 'the cool kids' behind the Scout hall in my hometown. I was in grade six and had the usual preteen pangs of wanting to fit in. However, even as I took that first drag of cigarette smoke with the horrid taste and the feeling of smoke entering my lungs, I took a step back and declared spontaneously to my 'cool kid' peers – "I'm not going to do this, I was only doing it to fit in." To my surprise, the 'cool kids' stopped and looked at me, then continued to take their next drag, accepting my decision without mocking me for being 'uncool'. Whilst I admit my act of defiance was no Rosa Parks, my right to choose and a hint of my values became cemented that day and my acceptance to own diversity became a whisper.

In looking back, I have attempted to determine who it was that role modelled feminine leadership and accountability to me, as I certainly didn't grow up with my parents teaching me about female heroes like Joan of Arc. During my adolescence, Thatcher, known as the Iron Lady, was made prime minister, and whilst that could have influenced my understanding that women could be in charge and influence change, the reputation of her that the media provoked suggested a style of country management that meant meeting her fellow masculine leaders with an equal, if not increasing, amount of the same energy.

My understanding is that there is a distinct difference in the definition of management and leadership. Leadership is listening, empowering and trusting in people; creating space for curiosity, mistakes, solutions and growth to arise, and showing up in that very same way. Management comes from practical thinking – getting things done through telling people what to do. It lacks opportunity for collaboration, ideas, growth and innovation, and often comes from the need to control fear as well as what could be perceived as an unsuccessful outcome. Sometimes we need management yet often we are lacking leadership in business.

There was also that time, whilst I clumsily sat on our coffee table (which, of course, was not for sitting on), that I scraped a big scratch in the wood, leaving an obvious sign that it was one of us kids, and when found out, I knew we'd be punished. It was a clear choice to own up; one that I met with a combination of fear and courage. I went up to my dad, spilled the beans and was waiting for the consequence by which he paused, took in his disappointment and said, "Nik, I'm so proud of you for owning up." Through this experience I learnt that it was okay to make a mistake and that on the other end of accountability is freedom and space for new learnings. I never sat on that coffee table again.

My mum, in her own right, demonstrated leadership to me, as she stepped into the role of single mum, working full-time and juggling the needs of four children. With longstanding health issues, she also showed a level of grace and resilience in doing her best to show up for us, her children, which I've come to learn is what we do as leaders. I remember once being on a panel with a group of small business owners and being asked for my thoughts on what defined good leadership, to which I responded, "Is there anyone in the room who is a parent?" Many hands went up, and I noted that being a leader is like being a parent – every day we get up attempting to be the best versions of ourselves and sometimes we make mistakes and sometimes we get messy. It's how we respond to this with our children that makes the difference.

A participant at this point put up his hand and asked, "So what do you do if you have had a bad day at work? Perhaps you've lost a sale or a client, and you become angry and take it out on your staff?"

To that I asked, "Well what would you do if that was your child?"

He responded, "I would reflect upon why I was so angry, apologise and think, then share how I may do things differently next time." As this dropped in, I could see the expression on his face change – he'd got it. Being a leader, like being a parent, does not mean being perfect; it means being self-aware and brave enough to be vulnerable. This experience heightened my understanding that often we see our journey as parents separate from our journey as leaders – yet if your parenting style is to encourage young humans to be empowered humans, then you probably have some transferable skills and experience to draw on when leading your individuals and teams.

As I've continued my entrepreneurial journey, there have been some very messy moments as I stumbled and redefined what impact I could make in allowing others to follow their own way or by paving a new leadership path with an aim to celebrate the humanness in leadership. I certainly feel my mum's legacy is intact as my resilience and grace (yes, even messy can be graceful if we let it) have too been challenged as I evolve on my leadership and parenting journey, bringing with me a new sense of wisdom along the way.

The influence of my parenting skills started at the age of nineteen when I fell in love with a man who had a two-and-a-half-year-old, and at that very moment of recognising that this was a very big deal, I had a choice to make. Do I embark on this new chapter with my newly formed family, knowing that without question for me, it will mean taking this on with my whole heart? Of course, I did. But being a 'just add water' mum at such a young age was clumsy and at times chaotic, as I was still being a child myself and had some heavy-duty unresolved trauma to dissect. She taught me so much about being vulnerable and being exposed to the hurt one feels when you love them unconditionally and you're in a situation where you're their safe place to vent, hurt and be held.

Mostly, she taught me the importance of showing up, how to create space to demonstrate being truthful when I'd made a mistake, and how to provide solutions and a purpose towards not making those same mistakes again, yet without shame attached. To be human, particularly in the messy parts. This would all later carve her path into her teens, particularly through those difficult years where pushing the boundaries and making mistakes were high on the agenda, as she would often reach out to me in times to work through these challenges, showing up vulnerable and beautifully messy in ways I'd shown her examples of through the years I'd parented her. Sometimes it was to problem-solve, other times it was to simply empower her to trust in her own ability to listen to what she needed to learn and grow, and at other times it was to just hold space without judgement. I recall her once coming to me in her early twenties feeling shame about a mistake she had made, and my words to her were, "You are barely twenty, and so much growth happens between twenty and thirty. Give yourself the permission to make as many mistakes as you can, and learn and grow from them."

Little did I know that big growth doesn't just happen in your twenties and thirties. It continues, if you dare it to, if you have an entrepreneurial spirit and a desire to lead wholeheartedly. You will push the boundaries and the norms and you will fall hard at times, because taking risks is sometimes inviting failure. And when falling/failing happens, it's often messy and can sometimes be painful. It can bring up old feelings of shame and sometimes guilt, and if we let it, we can get caught up in the narrative that failing/falling is bad, especially if we were taught (as many of us were) that making a mistake is wrong. However, I believe and have borne witness to many people who have sat with curiosity at their mistakes, both personally and professionally, and when they used it as an opportunity to learn and feel safe in having made a mistake – that's where growth happened. There is no shame in failure.

In my mid twenties, working as a law clerk in a law firm, the whisper to lead got louder as I put up my hand for a promotion to lead a team of eight. At the time, the itty bitty shity committee (IBSC) were challenging me in my head, shouting, *What are you doing? Are you crazy? You have never led anyone!* and *What do you know about leadership?* The CEO who accepted my application was the first I could say in my professional career who actually demonstrated leadership. He himself was the first CEO that the law firm had hired, and his role, partly by default, amongst a team of legal professionals, was to convince the critics that a CEO could be valuable to the business. He quickly won respect with his humble down-to-earth approach, combined with his strong business acumen. His ability to let me take full reign and learn as I go, asking questions and listening for my response as I problem-solved various challenges, was profound. What possessed me to put up my hand for this role, I can only say was my intuition and a desire to make a difference. I inherited those who had been challenged with a lack of morale thus impacting their productivity. I was studying HR at the time and was reading quite a lot of appropriate team-building theories, yet when I look back on those moments in my first leadership role, my success in building the morale and business efficiency had less to do with the theory and more to do with trusting my intuition and showing up as a fellow human. I earned respect from my diverse team members by showing up, listening, learning from and treating them as individuals, supporting their growth the best I knew how. In turn, I earned the respect of my peers and internal stakeholders by simply believing in my team, leading by example and owning up when things went 'wrong', which in turn spoke volumes in terms of the enhanced level of service our team provided. I didn't know it at the time, and I lacked confidence in its capacity to influence, yet I was onto something. By just bringing in my nurturing, feminine leadership style, I was making an impact.

I recall a few years after my promotion, as I departed for maternity leave, I shared in my farewell speech that I'd be back in six months because that's what I thought I needed and wanted – a career in a law firm, my true definition of success – or was it? I shared that my goal was to come back to my role as team leader, having enhanced my nurturing leadership style through my experience of being a mum. For many years I looked back at that moment and thought it was lame, after searching the faces of my peers, lawyers, supporting staff, fellow leaders and my own team members, looking for some kind of resonance on their faces. The challenge was that I believed in and was demonstrating flickers of wholehearted leadership back then, but no-one I knew was yet talking about leadership from that perspective.

The birth of my daughter brought an instant change to my mindset around what success could look like, yet I hadn't reconciled this by the time I returned to work after my committed six-month maternity leave. However, I had a symbolic moment the day before my return, looking at my work clothes and recognising how my body shape had changed and how the clothes (the costumes) no longer fitted. Yet that was not all that had changed. In those six months of embracing my feminine and nurturing attributes, the world of business looked different. I felt different. I also realised that I now had a responsibility to be a role model to a child; a daughter who looked to me, and who, through my actions, would be taught to be brave. My values had shifted, yet with the undue pressure on myself to conform to my old view of success and to be a leader in a traditional law firm with a large proportion of masculine counterparts, I felt like an imposter, and I was. There has been a lot written about faking it until we make it and bluffing our way through, and whilst faking and stepping out when you lack confidence can be wonderful validation, if faking is hindering your enquiry or growth to bring out your own unique superpowers (and in this case it was my nurturing leadership style), then faking will not have you make it with any sense of empowerment.

It would be years later when a fellow team member from that very same law firm reached out to me and said, "I need you. I have gone out on my [business] own, and I've hired on skills yet not on culture, and by the way, let's start a business together." When I asked him what he wanted this culture to look like, he replied with, "Unlike any other law firm." With that, the world of creating something different and something more authentic to his and my values became a possibility. To him, I am forever grateful – he saw the entrepreneur in me, he demonstrated possibility, and mostly he taught me that we don't need to cookie-cut to be successful. And to this, the lioness within me roared a little louder, yet not quite yet loud enough.

The road back to finding me after what I can only describe as cracking right open, was to truly reclaim the uniqueness of me – the messy and the vulnerable, and shedding the cookie-cutter version of myself – with equal amounts of pause and reflection time. Soon after this pause and reflection and harnessing my authentic self, a team member who I had led in those early days of my leadership journey reached out and shared with me, "Nikki, I would not be in business today if it wasn't for your leadership and your support in me following my path." It was then that I realised I was on to something … This time the lioness' roar was louder and prouder, because she could own her story wholeheartedly and create space for others to own theirs.

I'm not saying this part of the journey has been loaded with cartwheels and pretty parasols – leadership is often not easy. I have frequently been met with puzzlement form those managers who have not quite understood the importance of head and heart in equal measure. Yet the change in mindset happens on their time, and when I sit in my belief that I can influence wholehearted change, I allow them to pause and reflect, and puzzlement soon turns into a sense of curiosity. Furthermore, the more I seek to align myself and my business with those businesses, leaders and start-ups who have a sense that we can do business in a healthier way (where individuals and businesses thrive), the more impact I make.

For many leaders, entrepreneurs, creators of startups and those with an intrinsic desire to contribute and impact the world in a positive way, wholehearted leadership may start with the journey with themselves. Owning our own journey and our authentic self demonstrates wholehearted leadership and mostly it will be found in the ability to listen more, create space for pause and reflection, and spend a little less time responding to the traditional way of working. I trust my story will assist others to listen to their whisper and not wait a minute longer to trust in their wholehearted leadership journey; the world needs more of us.

Nikki Domeney

I'm Nikki, a free-spirited (perhaps because of my indigenous roots) entrepreneur, and director of H2O People & Culture. I have been in business for thirteen years, and in that time I've ridden the waves of the highs and lows, growth and challenges. My aim is to humanise the workplace on a global scale. I lead by example from my strong sense of intuition and bring an authentic wholehearted approach when working with humans in business and sharing my superpowers, whilst holding space for my fellow humans to find theirs. I believe if we create a safe space for people to be seen, heard and vulnerable, then we create opportunity for freedom and growth, which brings stronger clarity to identify our superpowers and ability to contribute our uniqueness to the world.

I grew up in the corporate world, yet never fitted the traditional corporate structure. Over time I understood it was less about me fitting in and more about it not fitting me. In business, I assist owners of business, leaders and team members to determine their values and I assist them in staying accountable. I am also a mum, which goes hand in hand with my leadership style, as I create a nurturing space for humans to be seen, be curious and grow. My intention for this book is to take you on a journey. I have something to say which I believe can impact the world of business, one that encourages females to lead from their feminine space and for their fellow male peers to equally benefit from experiencing their feminine colleagues; all with an aim to create more balance, harmony and healthier workplaces. I believe I am about to embark on a very personal journey, as showing up in this space to date has required a large dose of courage. I am leaning in and I'm ready to embrace this next chapter of my leadership and entrepreneurial journey.

LinkedIn: www.linkedin.com/in/nikki-domeney-91441058
Facebook: www.facebook.com/nikki.domeney.1

Printed in Australia
AUHW021248251121
356001AU00003B/3

9 780645 323009